Dear

Nephew

Letters of advice on
Dating
for Young Men

Tio Edwin

To Alex and Andru, my OG nephews. So you can be a better example to your siblings than I was to mine.

Faithful are the wounds of a friend... —Proverb 27:6

When I was a boy of 14, my father was so ignorant I could hardly stand to have the old man around. But when I got to be 21, I was astonished at how much the old man had learned in 7 years. —Mark Twain

Dear Nephew,

I've decided to write you a series of letters of advice. A desire to see you live a great life during your student years is my main purpose in these. I've just turned 40 this year; young enough to remember my student years, but old enough that I've had 20+ years to reflect upon my choices and see their outcomes. I will need to speak about myself if you are to learn from my mistakes and successes. It's also important for you to know the extent of my experience. My childhood was spent in Puerto Rico, my adolescence in rural Minnesota, I spent more than 14 years at University between my 4 degrees, and as a young man I took 5 trips to Europe, many to Central America and the Caribbean, and two to South America. This time at University and adventuring abroad exposed me to many different people and experiences. I would deeply regret not sharing what I've learned with you. You should know about the choices I made which have made my life infinitely richer, and you should have the benefit of hearing about my many mistakes so that you can avoid them. Proverbs 11:14 says, "Where no counsel is, the people fall: but in the multitude of counselors there is safety." I hope you will consider me one of your counselors, so that you can find your purpose and avoid some of the pit falls along the way.

I've walked down the road for 20+ years longer than you. I can look back and warn you about difficulties and characters you will meet along the way. My discipline gives me a unique vantage point as well. You see, I'm a musician. I've worked weddings, smoky bars, churches, and places you wouldn't want to meet your mother. I've played in the home of a multi-millionaire you'd recognize, been paid over a thousand dollars for playing two pieces, and I've also gotten paid with food. "Help yourself to casserole and coffee, and thank you for playing all afternoon." Being exposed to such a large cross-section of society has led to many interests which I hope you will at least consider during your educational years. I will keep my advice brief and to the point. Some topics will require more than one letter—perhaps many more. I will gladly spend the time needed to do each topic justice. You might be surprised by some of my advice. Sometimes the most sensible actions I took did not lead to my most fulfilling or profitable experiences. If I could go back, sometimes I would not do the most sensible thing. Most people give advice out of fear. I will not do that to you. I will look back at my own experiences and ask "what if I could go back and do it over? What things am I glad about? What things would I change, and what things would I keep the same?" Whenever a young person is cut off from their past (by not having a father, for example), in order to learn new things they must necessarily make mistakes that multitudes have made before them. Your life will be much richer and smoother if you learn from the mistakes of others. You will be hard pressed to find someone who has been a student longer, in more places, and in as many different circumstances as I have. So please learn from my mistakes and triumphs; have an open mind and a willingness to face the unknown. You have so many options in front of you. They say that youth is wasted on the young, but I hope that won't be the case with you. I want you to have an exciting, fulfilling life. I mean to talk to you about many topics: your career, money, travel, how you should approach your studies and how to make the best of them, how to prioritize your spiritual life, and many other things. I will begin with one of the most important topics in life that rarely gets the serious attention it deserves: women. The romantic relationships you pursue and establish will be among the most defining things in your life. The topic deserves more than jokes or whatever you might learn from strangers on the internet, so this will be the first topic we will cover. Please don't hesitate to write back with your opinions, comments, or questions. I will always love hearing from you and will always be.... Your affectionate uncle, Tio Edwin.

First say to yourself what you would be, and then do what you have to do.—Epicurus

God gives us all things at the price of labor.—Leonardo da Vinci

Dear Nephew,

Let's address a few things about you as a single man. As men we are seen by society from a utilitarian point of view. We are valued for what we provide. There's an old joke: women are human beings, men are human doings. Whether this is right or wrong is an interesting question, but we must deal with the world as it is. Women are seen as intrinsically valuable because they can give birth. This is why traditionally women and children are saved during times of tragedy. As young, able-bodied men, society expects us to help, not to need help. As a young man your first concern needs to be what you do for money. Thankfully your parents have taught you how to work hard and get along well with others. That's 80% of what's needed for steady income. Nobody gets ahead alone. Even if you start your own business selling something on the internet and don't need co-workers or employees, recurring business comes from customers liking you. The nice thing about having your own business is that if you lose a customer, you can hustle and find others. As an employee, make a mistake with a co-workers or, even worse, your boss, and you won't get many other chances. This is the main reason why being your own boss is so appealing. Office politics, jabs and insults from a boss who has power over you— it gets old. I suggest a two-pronged approach to avoid a lack of choices in the future: foster your passions while you experiment with different forms of income now. You have chosen to study for a career. As long as you can avoid massive amounts of debt, I congratulate you for this. As you know, I spent 14 years in college between my 4 degrees, and I don't regret a day spent at University. However, I wish I would have considered how I was going to make money as a musician. I was told to "follow my passion," so that's what I did, but I didn't stop and contemplate how my passion was going to feed my family. If you do have a passion, pursue it wholeheartedly. College is the perfect place for this. Your conversations with peers and professors will be a way to open your mind to many different career possibilities. While you are mainly focusing on your major—which should have something to do with your passions, of course— you should pursue ways of making money right now. Having a part time job would be a way to start, but I know you've had part time jobs before. Start thinking of ways you could make money that don't depend on a job. Can you put up posters or advertise yourself for a service you are good at providing? Lawn mowing, tutoring, carpentry, or anything of that sort? If there is absolutely no service you could provide right now, consider studying to become a plumber or electrician while you attend your college classes. It will be hard, but those are jobs that will always be needed. Lastly, tailor as much college work as you can towards future income. A book is a product that can be sold in the future. Have you noticed the amount of classes that have you write papers? I self-published two books by compiling research papers from different classes. Whenever asked to write a paper, I would write about a topic that I could compile into a book later on. This is the type of action that I want you to start taking consistently now. Worry about making an income, especially while you are still in school. Focus on it like a laser. There are a few reasons why this will quickly bring about positive changes in your dating life. Real self-esteem, your ability to provide, exposure to different social circles, and gained knowledge from your pursuits will all make you a more attractive and competent man. There are no shortcuts in life for anything. Mozart had a father who made him practice from the age of 3, so that by the time he was 13 he had avoided and overcome all the mistakes the father had learned over a lifetime. Competence and practical achievement are important for you financially, but they are the only way to create real confidence, which is attractive to women. Is being attractive to the opposite sex important as a young person? Yes it is. I will discuss why in a future letter. With warm regards from your affectionate uncle, Tio Edwin.

Keep away from people who try to belittle your ambitions. Small people always do that, but the really great make you feel that you, too, can become great.— Mark Twain

Live so that your friends will get bored when you die.—Julius Caesar

Dear Nephew,

A lot of people hate their job, but most love to play games. This is an interesting observation as games have a lot in common with work. There is a time commitment involved, repetitive tasks, and often difficult tasks to achieve. Failure is common in both, and a need to overcome obstacles in order to reach a goal. Depending on the job and game being compared, there might be no difference at all. One person might have a hobby of building a log home—essentially turning the endeavor into a game—while another might be employed doing the same thing and hate every minute of it. We all enjoy different games, especially the ones that put us in a state of flow. This useful concept was made popular by Mihaly Csikszentmihalyi in his book "Flow," published in 1990. The idea is that the state of Flow is one where we are challenged to our maximum potential in an activity that is possible for us to master. Athletes often call this being in "the zone." Runners call it "breaking through the wall." When we are in this state, we forget about ourselves and are completely immersed in the task at hand. The challenge is enough to keep us engrossed in the task, but doable enough that we can achieve it. Athletes who push themselves to break their last record, musicians completely focused during a concert, a novelist who wakes up from a writing session after sitting down to create a new world on paper— examples of ways to reach flow are as varied as there are people on the planet. Csikszentmihalyi argues that reaching this state on a regular basis is essential for happiness. Accomplishment is important, which explains why games can be so enjoyable to so many. From board games, video games, social games, and even the Olympics, games are universal. Video games are often organized in levels so that a player can master new skills and concepts before moving on to the next challenge. Csikszentmihalyi called flow the "secret to happiness" and play as "the flow experience par excellence." Contrast this with how most jobs work. In many, repetitive tasks are done without any concept of growth or purpose. Having to satisfy a boss encourages looking busy while avoiding risk. Rather than having the freedom to experiment, explore, and test oneself to see how much could be achieved, the incentive of traditional work is for workers to ingratiate themselves to their boss while not rocking the boat. A more soul-numbing endeavor is hard to find. I suspect that most successful entrepreneurs have found a way to make a game out of making money. In my own life, the jobs I've created for myself that I've enjoyed have many aspects of game play. At one point I started a series of salsa lessons where I treated advertising for it as a game. I began experimenting with different forms to see which one would be more successful. The entire experience took me years to reach a level of competence. Amazingly, I was able to pay my mortgage with the income from lessons in my small home studio. It was a wonderful experience. Importantly, it was a job I created for myself in which I had total freedom to improve, explore, experiment, and make my job essentially a game where the reward for leveling up was making more money. After this experience I took several University positions and traditional jobs with bosses. This seemed more secure—the grown up thing to do. As I was starting a family, the need for health care benefits trumped the need for autonomy. If I could go back, I would keep both a traditional job and my own "side hustle" where I'm free to explore and challenge myself without the approval of a boss. He who pays the piper, calls the tune, but sometimes it's nice to play without needing permission. While I hope you take your life and yourself seriously, I pray you'll begin to think about merging the worlds of work and play until they are indistinguishable from each other in your life. The only way women (or family and friends for that matter) will enjoy being around you is for you to enjoy your life. Work is such a big part of our life as men that this needs to be a priority for you now. Start brainstorming today. Make a list of the hobbies and games you love. Love playing a video game? What specifically do you love about it? Be as specific as you can. Once you can isolate what you love about it, you can begin the journey of finding work that also has that component you love. If you have any questions, don't hesitate to ask… your affectionate uncle, Tio Edwin.

We should look for someone to eat and drink with before looking for something to eat and drink.—Epicurus

He who finds a wife finds a good thing, and obtains favor from the Lord.— Proverbs 18:22

Dear Nephew,

Why should you worry about what women think about you, anyway? There is a current movement on the internet that encourages men to give up on marriage. While most of the people in this sphere offer some great help for young men, I sense that their overall premise is wrong. Of course, if we in our family had no faith, then I would agree wholeheartedly and say marriage is not an advisable gamble. However, we are a family of faith; we come from a religious people. Shunning marriage is not for us. Marriage is not only a sacrament, but it's the main way we continue our family line and heritage. We are proud of our ancestors —where they came from, the sacrifices they had to make to get us where we are, their hopes and dreams for us— we cannot in good conscience purposely break the chain of culture we inherited. Our lineage is too great for that, and our respect for our ancestry too strong. Granted, the laws of this country have become a nightmare for men's rights. Most marriages will end in divorce (mostly initiated by women) and women are always assumed to be angels in relationships while men are the assumed demons or idiots, depending on the circumstance. Especially since you're a man "of color" (as the cool kids say now), you'll notice that we are the assumed transgressors if any relationship conflict should arise. If a woman chooses to kill your child before the child is born, you have no legal recourse. While the traditional culture we come from defined gender roles each to be honored, in most of the West the father's role has been reduced to nothing but providing money. If the government can send checks, then the father's role is reduced to nothing. For those who have abandoned religion and tradition altogether, they are left with the unfortunate position of having to negotiate everything with their partner along every step of the way. A relationship is hard enough when there are clear rules and expectations. We see what happens to society when we become too sophisticated for the rules developed over thousands of years. This isn't to romanticize the past. If you knew half of the stories that your great-grandmother had to go through with your great-grandfather, you wouldn't believe they stayed married. But that underscores the point. In spite of all their troubles, they had a sense of religious and familial duty that kept them from breaking up the family. They did the best they could with the tools they had. Currently, society has decided to ignore the abundance of tools at our disposal both for finding love, and for staying happy while married. As I've already mentioned, this is not for us. If we are to have a fulfilling life, marriage is our default goal. There is always a possibility you might stay single, but we shouldn't expect that. You should proceed assuming that you will be married and have children. We honor our inheritance, we know we have a lot to give, and we want to have children and continue our rich family line. Tying yourself to the wrong woman can be a disastrous decision for both you and your children. Your choice of wife is one of the most important decisions you will make. I will discuss what to look for in women in future letters. For now, let's continue focusing on you. This is because you must have something to give before you seek to receive. Most young men focus on the feelings that the women around them make them feel. While this will eventually be important too, it is not the most important aspect of relationships you should focus on, especially at first. For now, you must make yourself someone who is worth following and spending time with. For now, just remember that the way women around you see you is important. We honor marriage and want it for ourselves. Finding the adequate woman to marry is very important. In order to do that, you must have relationships with women and worry about what they think of you right now so that you can attract and keep the right one for you. It's as simple as that. This week, ask a woman in your life who you are comfortable with to honestly tell you what aspects are attractive and which ones you could work on. If you don't have a female friend to ask, don't worry. This is a problem we will tackle in a future letter. With warm regards from your affectionate Uncle, Tio Edwin.

We fear the future because we are wasting today. —*Saint Teresa of Calcutta*

Keep away from people who try to belittle your ambitions. Small people always do that, but the really great make you feel that you, too, can become great. — *Mark Twain*

Dear Nephew,

When women are asked what they're attracted to, confidence always comes up. That and "he makes me laugh." Aristotle said courage is the virtue that makes all others possible. This is important to internalize. You will have options in life in proportion to your courage. No matter what ideas you might have; no matter what people you meet; no matter what opportunities you have; if you don't have the courage to risk failure, nothing will happen. Without courage, no dream can come true. Think of anyone you admire; the main thing you admire about them is their courage. How do we foster courage in ourselves? One small decision at a time. When I was a teenager, I was scared of beautiful females—something normal for teenage boys. Every time I suppressed that desire to approach a girl I felt worse about myself. While I was never visibly awkward about it, the internal struggle was enormous. As men you know that attraction for us is mostly visual at first, and it can be very strong. Just one look at a beautiful girl can make you obsess about her. We will want to speak with her, but fear sets in. What if she rejects you? As you've undoubtedly experienced, many females are experts at verbally hurting others. Pain from words can be brutal. I don't know where I got the idea to confront my fear of beautiful women head on, but I decided that every time I felt an attraction to a female, I would walk straight up to her, open my mouth, and say something. I ended up doing this for months. At first my interactions were very forced. I would unexpectedly sit right next to someone reading and say, "so… you're reading a book?" I tried my hand at different pick up lines. "Hey, did it hurt…. when you fell from the sky?" That type of cringy thing. After a few weeks, I learned the best thing to say was, "Hi! I don't believe we've met before. I'm Edwin. What's your name?" In other words, I treated them like normal people. I stayed friends with some of the women I met this way for years. Before I had gone through this exercise, I had unconsciously equated physical beauty with inner beauty. Unfortunately, this is rare. In fact, it seems like inner and outer beauty are more often than not inversely correlated. After some months of this exercise, I was approaching women by habit. The last month or so it was more of a chore, as I had enough friends and really felt no need to be meeting more people—girls in particular. The last few times I approached a beautiful woman I went up with my usual introduction, said "well, nice to meet you," and just walked away. I'm sure I offended one or two females who questioned why I would even introduce myself and then just walk away. At that point, I decided to stop. I had gained the confidence I desired the only way that confidence can be built: through achievement. Real confidence and self-esteem is only found after you decide to do something, fail, and persist until it is achieved. Failure will be part of the journey, but pushing through the negativity will make your end goal more rewarding. To become more confident, find something that you are afraid of and work every day to overcome that fear. If your fear is related to women, even better, because overcoming this fear will be a crucial step in finding the right woman. If you have never tried this exercise in your own life, I would suggest starting today. Every time you feel that drive to go speak with a beautiful woman, if circumstances allow it, go up to her and introduce yourself. You will soon find that a woman being beautiful doesn't mean she is a great person, or even someone who might be worth talking to for you. Most importantly, you will discover there is nothing to be scared of as your self-confidence continues to grow. This is by no means the only fear to overcome, of course. Find what you fear, and make a simple plan to overcome it. Achievement is the only way to foster the confidence women intuitively look for, so get to work in overcoming your fears and achieving real goals in your life. With warm regards from your affectionate uncle, Tio Edwin.

Appreciation is a wonderful thing. It makes what is excellent in others belong to us as well.—Voltaire

Art is the queen of all sciences, communicating knowledge to all the generations of the world.—Leonardo do Vinci

Dear Nephew,

As a young student, you must focus on being the best bachelor you can be. Making money and conquering your fears start you on the road to improving yourself in tangible ways. Focus on these two goals as best you can, but don't forget there is more to life. On top of being a provider, a man must give a woman companionship. This means having interesting hobbies as well as being a good conversationalist. Just like music, conversation is an art form everybody thinks they are great in, but very few actually are. An artist must have something to say before being able to say it through their medium. This is why on top of the goals you have set out for yourself, you must learn about the world as much as you can. Travel, discover new hobbies, read, watch films. As long as they aren't immoral, don't shy away from new experiences. Storytelling is a key component of good conversation. How can you tell good stories if you've never lived them? The more open you are to new people and experiences, the more knowledge you will have about the world, making you an increasingly interesting, attractive person. This is key. There are lots of courses and gurus out there that teach pick up lines and "game" in order to be more appealing to women. While some of this material can be helpful, realize that you can't always be performing. If your goal is to pick up a girl at a bar for a one-night stand, then these methods would be fine, but that is not your goal. You are looking to meet a quality girl that will make an incredible wife, mother, and new family member. There is really no end to the number of extracurricular pursuits that you could take an interest in, making the search for hobbies a very rewarding one. These pursuits can last for your entire life. Besides the ones I've already listed for you, I would like to encourage you to take up social dancing. From personal experience, this activity will change your life. I'm not talking about clubbing, where people mostly either simulate sexual activity on the dance floor in front of strangers, or stand in a circle with friends, awkwardly gyrating random parts of their bodies in a somewhat related tempo to the music. I tried this for a while as a young man and, trust me, if you never do it you aren't missing anything. The whole activity is rather sad and embarrassing, actually. Of all the times I went clubbing, I only have one good memory with two amazing female friends. I hope I remember to tell you that story in the future. No, the type of dancing I'm talking about is partner dancing. You know: waltz, foxtrot, swing. Partner dancing is a wonderful activity that will enlarge your social circles and your sphere of interest immensely. It's a physically demanding activity and an art form. Besides helping you stay in shape, you learn about music, history, and social etiquette. As you know, I've been a Latin dance teacher for almost 20 years, and I have loved it. This doesn't mean that it's always easy. Whenever there are social dynamics at play (as there are in any group) there will be negative moments, people who bother you, and others who will not improve your life. On the whole, however, those who take up social dancing are adventurous people who love connecting with others in a personal way. There is nothing quite like the feeling of dancing well with someone. It's truly an achievement worth going for that will render many returns on the time invested. So try everything: travel, languages, movies, cooking and food, history or literature clubs, the visual arts, social speaking clubs, but most importantly, dance. I'll expand upon dancing a bit more in my next letter. For now, go to www.meetup.com and start searching for clubs and activities near you that you think you might enjoy. See if you can find something for the next week or two.

With warm regards from your affectionate uncle, Tio Edwin.

A person's worth is measured in the worth of what he values.—
Marcus Aurelius

Not what we have but what we enjoy, constitutes our abundance.
—Epicurus

Dear Nephew,

Give social dancing a try. You will be surprised by the needs it fulfills in your life. We are created to live in community, yet live quite isolated lives. We need human contact, and not just social contact, as important as that is. Physical, skin-to-skin contact with other human beings is rare. Once a massage therapist traded massages for dance lessons with me. I will be forever grateful to that woman. After a few sessions, I realized how much I had been missing in life. It wasn't just a physical benefit. Emotionally, I left each massage ready for anything; my body having internalized acceptance and caring. To a lesser degree, this is achieved in dance. Before dancing, I make sure I'm groomed and pleasant to be around: teeth brushed, deodorant on, with practical clothing. I have to consider how I will be perceived. When I arrive, it is expected that I will approach women if I want to dance. It will take me at least a few lessons to feel confident enough for this; I will have earned that confidence through real achievement. Every time I approach a woman to ask for a dance (even if I know her) there is a chance that I will be rejected. I must overcome this fear of social rejection in public. I won't get rejected every time, but when I do, I learn to take a woman's rejection gracefully, without feeling bitter or angry. I will internalize that nobody owes me a dance. Besides, I don't know her situation right now. She might be tired, need to take a break—it could be anything. If she says yes to dancing reluctantly, the dance won't be good anyway. I knew a woman who never wanted to dance with me because she was insecure about how tall she was. As a very short man, I would make her look even taller, and she didn't want that. I had to accept it, to her loss; some of the funnest, most memorable dances I've had were with a woman who was 6'7". Once I find someone to dance with, I become aware of my body, something we seldom do. My brain gets an incredible work out as I make calculations about my moving body in relation to another moving body. Social dancing is such a tough mental workout, in fact, that it's physical exercise that helps ward off dementia. Look it up. Our skin is touching, and we are very close, acknowledging the presence and importance of another person. As men, we are the assumed leaders of each dance, so we make decisions the entire time. After mastering this skill, a man becomes used to thinking one step ahead; without that constant forethought and planning, no dancing is possible. I trust I don't need to mention how perfectly this habit of mind applies to your dating life. Besides the connection between me and the women I dance with, I need to be aware of how the other men are leading their partners on the floor. This skill is known as floor craft. Without good floor craft, crashes often happen between couples. The subtle acknowledgement of other men and their skills will lead to an admiration of better dancers. Hopefully real friendships arise with other male dancers as well. On top of all the emotional, inner work, if I dance salsa for a couple of hours, I've taken around 10,000 steps, the daily amount recommended for good health but one that we seldom reach in modern society. Social dancing is a full physical, mental, and social workout. Like an old mentor of mine used to say: if you are naturally shy around girls, all you need to say in order to start a friendship is "may I have this dance." Besides a fun way to meet women, social dancing is a great way to improve yourself. Try out your nearest studio. Whether it's ballroom, swing, Latin, or Renaissance dance, you won't regret taking this step in your life. This letter barely scratches the surface of the benefits you will gain from learning to partner dance. Not all learning is book learning. With warm regards from your affectionate uncle, Tio Edwin.

Live so that your friends will get bored when you die.—Julius Caesar

A career is wonderful, but you can't curl up with it on a cold night.— Marylin Monroe

Dear Nephew,

Make money, conquer your fears, and try everything. Those are my first three pieces of advice for you in a nutshell. Once you reach a place where you feel you're making personal progress in these areas, then start to shift the focus from yourself to the women around you. After all, the goal is being able to offer a woman a wonderful improvement in her life by being with you. How do you know you are interested in someone? Notice what I ask here. I didn't ask you, "how do you meet someone?" If you have followed my previous advice and are living an active, fruitful life meeting your goals, you will be meeting more girls than you know what to do with. In fact, your main problem will be learning to say "no" to engagements, as you also need to rest and have time alone. If you do find yourself feeling alone, then you aren't focusing enough on others and the world outside yourself, which should include those interests, fears, and goals of making money previously mentioned. This is a key point I don't want you to miss. When I was young, I used to have a little black book with names of girls I would call if I was feeling lonely or sad. I would simply call the list and make plans with anyone who could go out with me immediately. I regret doing this for so long. I wish I could tell my younger self that female companionship wasn't what I was craving, ultimately. Sure it's nice at the moment, and it gives you someone to talk to and have fun with, but it was time I could have devoted to improving myself in those three areas of Money, Fears, and Interests. Typically I would end up spending money on a random female that I had no intention of marrying, dating, or sometimes even seeing more than a few times. I dated so many girls when I was a young student that I've even forgotten the names of a few that became my girlfriends. If that is not the jargon used anymore by the cool kids, that means we were in an exclusive, romantic relationship and not seeing anyone else for months. I've dated at least two women from every continent on earth (except Australia). While I'm glad I was open to the experiences, I do regret all the time and especially money spent on wining and dining these ladies. I made a rough calculation, and my conservative estimate is that I probably spent at least $300,000 on dating women when I was a young student. This calculation doesn't include gas, presents, or time wasted. Talk about a poor investment. I was spending all my money on women. While some were great company, most wouldn't even remain friends after I stopped paying for their time. Of course, not everything is about money, but that sentiment should go both ways. If you don't know a girl well-enough to know if she is worth the financial sacrifice to treat her to something special, don't spend money on her. That trip on the ferry that promises to be so romantic will not turn out the way you think it will if you don't know anything about the girl. If there is chemistry between you, you will be able to feel it even if you are cleaning toilets in a nursing home with an octogenarian in the next stall. Don't think it's your job to impress her now. It isn't. It's your job to become the best person you can be for your own sake and for the sake of your future wife and children. While doing this personal work, evaluate the women around you to see who you admire. Having worked on yourself and conquered your fears, you are now able to approach and befriend any woman who attracts you physically. Having many female friends and acquaintances isn't a great achievement. The real achievement is being able to know what specifically you want in a woman, learn to spot it, and be able to attract that specific person. We will turn our attention to this task in the upcoming letters. Always wishing you the best in life, your affectionate uncle, Tio Edwin.

Only two things we'll regret on deathbed — that we are little loved and little traveled.
—Mark Twain

We never live, we are always in the expectation of living.—
Voltaire

Dear nephew,

If you are able to travel and date women from other cultures, please do it. Many cultures don't have the same concept of dating that we do, so it's important not to assume intentions or how the relationship should proceed. It is helpful to have a broad idea of how women around the world expect romantic relationships to develop since underlying assumptions vary greatly. I enjoy how ritualistic American culture is in dating. Picking a girl up, taking her to dinner, paying for the meal, driving her back—there's an expectation to be fulfilled. Do these rituals and it will be assumed that you're starting a relationship. This isn't the case everywhere. In parts of Western Europe, even if you spend time together, it will be assumed that you are not in a relationship until openly discussed and decided upon. In my experience, Mediterranean women are more open to possible relationships. It seems like dating isn't seen as such a permanent, important thing, so breaking up doesn't mean people can't be friends. Germans and northerners seem to have attitudes more like North Americas, where dating has more social significance. West African cultures are very aggressive romantically, I have experienced; it could be jarring. Once you understand this, however, dating a West African woman could be a wonderful thing. I briefly went out with a girl from Ghana. After going out once, she wanted me to commit exclusively. There are two words we use in romance: like and love. This is partly why committing can be such a hard thing for us. In her Ghanaian language, she had 16 different words to denote romantic interest in 16 different gradations of intensity and commitment. Of course she could be upfront about her feelings! In her mind, she was telling me she liked me at that starting level. There can be 15 more levels to go, and you usually get married around the 10th level of that spectrum. Very helpful in terms of love, West African languages. I got scared from that relationship, something I came to regret. Traditional cultures in Latin America will have very distinct gender roles that can make life easier. Who cooks, who tries to make money, who disciplines the kids and how; those are issues that don't have to be fought over. Latin American women are beautifully feminine, too. Most of them will be very touchy-feely with you, dress to impress, and give you a special place as a man. Even with "feistier" Latin cultures such as Puerto Ricans or Cubans (as opposed to more traditional cultures in Peru or Guatemala), women will very often serve you meals, for example, to show they care about you. It feels wonderful to have frequent gestures of respect and care from a woman, gestures that North American women seldom give. Asian women are seen as the holy grail to many Western men. I'm convinced this is due to several factors. First, notice how cute the typical East Asian face looks. The high cheek bones and flatter contour of the face is more youthful and child-like. While this doesn't help Asian men be seen as more masculine around the world—notice the many unfortunate and, frankly, racist portrayals of East Asian men in film—Asian women are perpetually seen as more feminine. On top of the advantages in physical beauty Asian women enjoy—the extra fat layer around the eyes prevents premature wrinkling, for example—East Asian cultures are also very different from Western cultures, adding a sense of exoticism. The Japanese emphasis on social harmony, order, and knowing your place would be an incredibly attractive lifestyle for a man divorced from an American woman who would belittle him in public and considered cooking and serving him a meal a sexist atrocity. I was communicating for about a year with a woman from Pakistan who was looking to have an arranged marriage. After some months of communication, she asked me to consider marrying her. It was quite an experience. Her parents had given her six months to find a husband, otherwise they would find one for her. We wrote back and forth for months, talked on the phone for a few weeks, and made plans to meet in London. She was willing to get married without ever having met, but I told her that, as a Westerner, it was too scary not to meet even once. I never went through with the trip, but we still keep in touch through a social network. She has a wonderful husband, kids, and I'm glad to have lived that experience thanks to her. I even communicated with her husband several times. There are many ways of dating, courting, and seeking a mate around the world. While the extra layer of complexity could be difficult to navigate, it is also incredibly rewarding to navigate through another culture in such a personal way. If you want to learn about another culture, the best way to do so is to date someone from that culture. The intimacy and insight into the person's life while dating cannot be replicated in an interaction with an acquaintance or casual friend. If you end up dating more than one person, I hope you will consider dating women from different cultures. You will not regret it. If you've never traveled abroad, it's time to start thinking about it today. Where would you go and why? How can you make that trip happen sooner than later? With warm regards from your affectionate uncle, Tio Edwin.

The secret of being a bore is to tell everything.—Voltaire

All you need in life is ignorance and confidence; then success is sure.—Mark Twain

Dear Nephew,

I had a very rewarding friendship with my friend Sam while doing my doctorate. He was a bit socially awkward—nothing extreme—but told me on several occasions that when it came to women, he was a master at repelling them. Physically speaking, we were around the same level of attractiveness, so I began to observe him wondering why this was the case. Our friendship grew to the point we were becoming vulnerable with each other, so I asked him if he wanted to meet once a week in order to go over strategies for working on himself. I had observed several areas in himself which he could improve, and so I offered to help him with that if he would like. We only met for a few months for this reason, but it was wonderfully productive for both of us. The best way to learn is to teach, and while I knew the concepts I presented to him, I didn't really internalize them until I taught them. We met once a week at a local Denny's restaurant. Playing mind games to not get nervous or make women feel insecure so they value you are worthless tricks that aren't good for anyone. You can't possibly cover all possible scenarios and have witty one-liners ready. Besides, getting nervous is a natural part of life, not something wrong with you to be avoided. All we need to worry about is the art of conversation. We started practicing how to keep a conversation natural and flowing. I explained that making associations between items in a room and what they remind you of is the quickest way to always have some conversational topic at your disposal. I took a napkin, held it up as an example, and went through 10 quick associations. Napkin: paper, trees, leaves, wood, roots, water, river, ocean, boats, travel. If conversation slows, pointing out that napkin and making my association clear could lead our conversation from our table to the river freezing outside or international travel stories. To tell personal travel stories, it helps if you've traveled, but you get the point. Those associations are ways to always have conversational topics at hand. If you practice making quick associations between what you see right in front of you and completely separate items or events that they bring to mind, you will never run out of topics of conversation. When those associations become second nature, it's then a matter of practicing different ways of smoothly connecting the dots for other people from topic to topic. We began to practice. Sitting at one of the booths in Denny's during our first session, I asked him if he noticed anything that caught his eye in the room. He looked down and told me, "I noticed that steak knife." After saying this, he slowly looked up at me while quietly sustaining eye contact. I stopped him immediately and said, "Sam, you're creeping me out man. What in the world are you noticing about the knife?," I asked, a little nervous. "Well, it has a serial number on the side. That serial number reminds me of a similar one on the side of a World War II destroyer that had an incredible adventure with…" "Stop!," I told him. I cut him off because he had gone from creeping me out to absolutely fascinating me in a matter of seconds. It was amazing how much this guy knew and how hidden his personality would remain if he didn't work on ways of showing what a cool guy he was. After telling me the WWII story (which was truly fascinating), we continued practicing to make those associations. We played with skipping the connecting material and jumping from one topic to another to see how that felt to him personally. Conversation is a personal art form that will be unique to every human being, which is the beauty of connecting with other people. While conversation was our main emphasis, we also dealt with gestures, body positioning, and other small ways to communicate non-verbally. Months later, he met his future wife. He asked me to be one of his groomsmen and told me that, without my help, he would not have been able to share himself with his wonderful new bride. It filled me with happiness to realize our little get togethers helped him in such a big way. Human beings think through language, so verbally communicating with others is our main way of making connections and creating relationships. Make sure not to neglect the art of conversation. It's a fun challenge to find ways of expanding your conversational palette. This will be of personal benefit to you in any circumstance when speaking with others, but especially when seeking ways to connect with the women around you. Do you know any talented conversationalists in your social circles? Call him or her today and see if you can arrange to spend regular time together. Your affectionate uncle, Tio Edwin.

No man is free who cannot command himself. —*Pythagoras*

Some people think luxury is the opposite of poverty. It is not. It is the opposite of vulgarity. —*Coco Chanel*

Dear Nephew,

Lying is something we all do almost every day. We lie with words, with actions, with omissions. We lie without intending to, sometimes. We need to work against this habit, especially in relationships with the opposite sex. The best way to do this is to start noticing what qualities you appreciate in a woman. What is it that you want? Are you attracted to a girl who is ambitious and makes her own money? Is a girl that flirts with other men a deal breaker for you? Would it bother you if she went to the beach in a thong and became upset if you asked her not to show her anus in public? You need to understand how you feel about these situations. You are becoming quite an exceptional man, and quality men are rare. While large parts of our male population are either in jail or have simply given up on life, you have attributes and qualities that most women naturally find attractive. You are studying to better yourself, you have real, inner confidence without being arrogant because you have set goals for yourself and accomplished them. You have also started to experience more of life: traveling, learning, doing… You are an interesting person. Girls will be pursuing you. I know because it happened to me, to my amazement. I'm not an attractive man; far from it. I'm a 5-foot nothing, brown, slightly out of shape, hairy man that never had much money or game. I was more of a nerd than anything, but I set out early to conquer my fears and learn as much about the world as I could in order to be a good artist. Just those two things brought women into my life, and I found myself in social situations I never anticipated. You are taller than me and starting these self-improvements younger than I was. The fact that you're worried about making money as well will make you attractive, and this is why you must know what you want. If you don't, you'll say yes to any woman who wants to spend time with you romantically. She will invite you to her apartment, and since you don't want to be rude and aren't doing anything anyway, why not? After the 5th time of doing this, if she doesn't throw herself at you, she will more than likely begin romantic gestures. It's at this moment that you must know what you want. Don't just lie and go with the flow because it's easy. I've had girlfriends for long periods of time where the only thing I said was "sure" to start the relationship. Not wise. A relationship with a woman should move forward from your own initiative, not to comply with her. Don't lie and pretend you're married, dating, or even interested in someone when you're not. Every single woman has a body, and you will be attracted to 99% of those bodies. If you don't know you want a relationship with the person, don't go along with it and use your attraction to her body as an excuse to lie to yourself. An image of a woman on paper is attractive to men. Pornography is yet another factor that takes men out of the dating pool. The woman on the page or screen can't reject you, and you can see as many female bodies as you'd like. I suspect romantic relationships have declined in your generation because men opt for this lie over reality. Unfortunately, many women are willing to profit from these online venues and keep the supply flowing. It's a sad thing to see someone addicted to pornography, unable to have a relationship with a woman. If any of your brothers (or even sisters in some cases) struggle with this, never hesitate to offer them help and friendship. I've had several friends tell me they wanted to stop watching porn. Now that pornography is so ubiquitous, it might not be such an awkward subject for your generation. I hope so. To the best of your ability, don't lie to a woman. Know what you want, and if she isn't it, tactfully, but clearly let her know before she considers you a possibility for a relationship. If she approaches you and you don't know, tell her you don't know. You'll avoid a lot of wasted time and pain. With warm regards from your affectionate uncle, Tio Edwin.

Our wretched species is so made that those who walk on the well-trodden path always throw stones at those who are showing a new road —Voltaire

People of accomplishment rarely sat back and let things happen to them. —Leonardo da Vinci

Dear Nephew,

What does not lying to women look like in practice? There's a reason why so many people call dating a game. In social situations, there are unspoken rules. Dealing with these unspoken expectations will be most of your work in avoiding conflict. For example, if you hang around lots of other girls, you assume a woman will understand you are not interested in dating her exclusively. However, most women look for men that other females like as social proof they are safe. Every time you tell her about some problem with another girl, you believe your we're-just-friends message is clear. In her mind, she believes you're trusting her more and becoming more romantically interested. The signals you might be trying to send could be exactly the opposite in her mind. Most conflicts in your dating life will come from these unspoken assumptions. Some of the conflicts can be pretty harmless and even funny. I remember as a freshman feeling annoyed at walking outside while speaking with another person. Even if headed to the same place, there were always several paths to get there. Every time we reached a crossroads, both of us would slow down, assume different paths and diverge, or almost run into each other. Most of the time this would cause a chuckle, but it happened so often it annoyed me. I discovered that even while chatting, if I pointed in a direction before the crossroad, we would take the path I pointed to and avoid that awkward moment. This might seem insignificant, but it's those small gestures that make interactions and relationships go smoothly. At first I was fearful that a woman I walked with would feel offended at my non-verbal directions. Even though I did this with men as well, a man giving her overt instruction might seem sexist to her. It was exactly the opposite. Conversation could keep flowing without that awkward hesitation at every intersection. This small decision-making task I had assigned to myself also helped boost my confidence, as every time I did it I had to overcome my fear of offending the other person. Eventually, it became a practical habit and social consideration for me. However, it is also a good metaphor for how you can avoid lying to the women in your life. There will always be a million scenarios that can happen socially between people, so we can't possibly plan for them all. The best thing we can do is have clear principles to apply. While enjoying the company of a woman, you should always be the one who points to the next road you want to take with her, metaphorically speaking. You might come to a place where the road diverges. She might be headed straight for physical intimacy with you, thinking that's what all men want. Whatever her motivation, it needs to be you who decides which road you will take. Point to the road you want to take before you get there. While there might be several options to consider, your decision needs to be clear to yourself first. As the man in the relationship, set the pace and direction you are going in. It is far too easy for most of us to go along with whatever a woman wants and lie to ourselves about it. Just like I felt bad about pointing while walking with a girl, you might feel like you are offending a woman by not going along with everything she wants. "I can't believe you talked with her after I told you that she makes me jealous!" "I thought we were going to this movie alone!" These types of interactions are crossroad moments. The possible scenarios are endless, but the principle is the same. YOU decide which road you will be taking. Once you know, you can clearly communicate that. If you don't know, stand still and clearly communicate that. If she chooses to ignore you or get mad at your decisions, your paths will diverge soon enough as you keep walking forward. Don't worry. Even if you end up losing a few companions, your clear decisions will keep you on the path to better, more exciting things. If you ever have doubts as to which path is best, reach out to your parents, your family and, of course, … your favorite uncle, Tio Edwin.

Whatever it is you're seeking won't come in the form you're expecting—Haruki Murakami

Do not look back when leaving. —Pythagoras

Dear Nephew,

Most of us make many attempts at getting to know people, some that will not be compatible with us. It's part of life if we are to reach our goal of marriage. Now that you've leveled up as a single man, it's time to consider a woman in a more serious way. Study what you want. As you've been exploring the world and bettering yourself, you've seen what you don't want. That's a starting point, but only that. It's easy to know what to avoid, but what to pursue is another matter. The first step is to prune away the people you don't want in your life. As babies, the connections in our brain are completely open to other connections nearby. The way that we learn language and everything else is that those connections start to organize into networks. By narrowing their scope, those channels specialize for a specific language or task. That channel must reject connections with other circuits in order to work. You will be doing this with women in your life. You'll be discovering who you connect with and who makes you feel the magic in the world. This necessarily means rejecting the wrong women. One of the toughest things for us men to do is reject a woman who is after us romantically or sexually. We are taught from childhood to never upset a female. I recall getting physical with women for whom I had no attraction. She would make the first move, I wouldn't want to make her feel bad, so I'd go along. Only on one occasion did this not lead to needless drama. Avoid this situation at all costs. It will lead to awkwardness or pain that could be avoided by not giving in to temptation. When should you start this pruning process? It depends on when you want to get married. I would suggest getting married young. I got married as an older man, but I didn't gain much from avoiding marriage. My brother did the opposite and married quite young... he was barely 18, in fact. While our culture discourages that, if you have a good head on your shoulders and a deep, religious commitment to marriage, getting married young to a great woman is the best thing you could do. While my years of dating many women were not a complete waste of time, lessons learned and fond memories pale in comparison to the richness and fulfillment that a marriage gives you, even without children. When children come, everything else seems meaningless in comparison. You suddenly realize that, before you had them, your heart was smaller than the Grinch's. Your children need you to have a great relationship with your wife. This is why finding the right woman is important now, when you're young, not as an afterthought. I treated dating flippantly for too long; a great regret for me. This type of casual dating is not worth the cost. Save your money now and avoid the awkward, meaningless dates with girls you don't care to know. Only spend money on quality women that are marriage material. This means getting to know women in a meaningful way before jumping on the first step of the relationship escalator. It's risky enough getting on it even after careful consideration because the longer you stay, the higher you go and the more painful it is to jump off this escalator. In upcoming letters, I will share lessons I've learned from specific women I've dated and the stories I lived through with them. We have been speaking a lot about first principles and generalities, but I would like to show you how these principles apply to specific situations. Some of my stories will be examples of what to do, but I'm afraid most of them will be cautionary tales. I hope you will find the strength to avoid the many mistakes made for years by… your favorite uncle, Tio Edwin.

Every man is a creature of the age in which he lives and few are able to raise themselves above the ideas of the time. —Voltaire

*A man is never as big as when he is on his knees to help a child.
—Pythagoras*

Dear nephew,

One of the most toxic, childish, and selfish kind of people you want to avoid in dating (or letting into your life in general) are people who have decided they never want children. If they have thought it through and realize the implications of what they are doing and encouraging others to do, then we can add evil to that list of adjectives. However, most of these people haven't considered what they are saying and so I relegate their opinion to ignorance. It is the beginning of 2022 as I write this to you, and there is a renewed cultural interest right now for voluntary childlessness to be "normalized," like the cool kids say. A few weeks ago the Pope came out against this idea by calling people who choose not to have children "selfish." While this Pope is insufferably liberal beyond parody sometimes—you'll recall his derisory "Who am I to judge?" comment about gay marriage—on this point, of course, he is completely correct. Selfish is the kindest descriptor here. Keep in mind that we aren't talking about people who can't have children, or who want to wait and have children with the right person, or who want to adopt children rather than have their own. No, we are talking about adults who are perfectly capable of having children, who have romantic partners and are able to have children, but choose not to have children or adopt them. The lack of pride and respect for ones culture and family that must be attained to reach that conclusion borders on the repulsive; the hopeless attitude towards the future, bordering on the pathological; the lack of faith in themselves, beyond dismal. Picture the joy of a father teaching his son or daughter something new, showing them how much he loves them, and making that child feel loved, cared for, and safe. Picture a mother comforting a child when they cry, and teaching them that they are stronger than their pain. These countless, precious moments that must happen in order to mold a child become the most precious memories of ones life. Now imagine someone wishing they had never had these so that they could've had a bigger house, more chances to visit Disney World alone, or work on their super important career. We could conclude that there is something morally and perhaps cognitively wrong with this person; a sickness of the soul, perhaps. This is not surprising, once we consider the sources of this so-called cultural movement. Listening to a National Public Radio program on the topic, I heard caller after caller comment on how much they love their children but that, if they could go back, they would choose not to have them. NPR's audience is almost 90% white and college educated. If a culture is this sick, perhaps the compassionate response is to let it die. Let them abort all their children and perhaps euthanize themselves. White people in this country are the first to hate their "whiteness," and perhaps we should encourage them to end their culture so that our grandchildren don't have to suffer through their endless, vainglorious nonsense. Reassuring whispers of "Thank you for sharing. So brave," are not the appropriate response to someone telling the world that if they could go back they would not have their child, or just abort them. That's not sophisticated and brave. That's pathological, contemptible, and reminds me of why so many people around the world can't stand Americans, although everyone will take their money. You have brothers and sisters who have lighter skin than us, but light skin doesn't make you white in the cultural sense. There are plenty of light-skinned people from India, the Middle East, Asia, Northern Africa, Latin America, and other parts of the world that approximate the skin color of Northern European ancestry, but they wouldn't be considered white here. No, this particular tendency to disrespect your ancestry and see your culture destroyed seems to reside within Western white populations, American whites in particular. For their ability to buy extra video games and go on yet another Mediterranean cruise they are willing to give up on the most precious thing life this side of glory has to offer: family. Let the white population here go extinct if they choose. Like the old saying my mother used to tell me goes: "They are white, and they understand each other." For us, the default is marriage and children, and we are proud of it, because we are proud of our families, we are proud of our people, we are proud of where we come from, and we feel that it is a blessing to have our people on this planet, faults and all. Even if we aren't rich materially, we are rich in culture, life, tradition, and love. With warm regards from an uncle who's proud of you, Tio Edwin.

Don't be humble. You're not that great. —Golda Meir

Love begins by taking care of the closest ones — the ones at home. —Saint Teresa of Calcutta

Dear Nephew,

I asked a girl to be my first girlfriend when I was fourteen years old. I had seven official girlfriends that I dated for at least two years—some up to four. Besides that, I've had well over thirty romantic liaisons and "minor" girlfriends (girlfriends that I dated for only months). That means I've had more than 40 romantic relationships with different women in my life. This is amazing even to myself. If you were to look at me objectively, you would see a 5'-nothing, brown, hairy man with average looks. This illustrates how physical advantages are not as important as persevering over your challenges. I've had so many girlfriends in my life that I have sadly forgotten some of their names. I will never forget the girlfriends that I dated for years, of course, but I have forgotten the names of some that were briefly in my life. I will never forget their faces, though. I'm proud of the fears I overcame to approach women as a young man, and I wish I had written more down in journals to never forget important details. Even having forgotten some of their names, I hold them fondly in my heart as we shared some of the most beautiful moments in my life. Their names might elude me, but the memories are there. Unfortunately, I did waste a lot of time dating one girl at a time. These were mock-marriage relationships — a huge mistake and something I would change if I could go back. I should have never pretended to be married when I wasn't. Having girlfriends and going out with women is fun and I'm glad I did it, but I did it for too long. Simply following what everybody expected me to do was not a good idea. Nobody else could live my life for me, yet I decided to adhere to cultural norms and expectations, instead of discovering what I wanted. I'm not saying that I should have lied and cheated, because lying is wrong. I simply should not have dated exclusively, at least not until I knew the woman well. Until then, we could go out, hang out, and even call it dating for those around us. While dating, if I desired to spend time with another girl, I should have mentioned that and done it. Dating exclusively (a mock marriage), particularly when you are a student, is not a good idea. It is both a waste of time and a form of self-deception. It is dishonest to expect someone to be totally committed to you when there has been no declaration of fidelity. That needs to be a serious conversation, not something that is assumed. It took me years of dating to realize this. Even in more serious dating relationships, you are single until proven married. This is the best way to think about relationships with the opposite sex while being a student. In the West we typically date and form a relationship before getting married. For us it seems that parents are rarely involved in our dating decisions. After meeting a few women from the middle east that felt the opposite way—and considering marriage with one—I adamantly disagree with this approach. While the individualism of the U.S. (and the West more generally) is a great thing for many aspects of life, I believe it is a detriment for our romantic lives. If you are lucky enough to have grown up with a father and a mother—both who love you, have studied you your whole life, and know you better than you know yourself in some ways—why would you not accept their counsel and direction in this most important aspect of your life? Heck, if you have extended family, why not go to them as well (as you are doing now with your Tio)? I considered an arranged marriage with a girl from Pakistan at one point, and it was a wonderful experience. I ended up not pulling the trigger for a few reasons, but compared to other dating experiences I've had, it was truly uplifting and helped me grow as a person. I had to figure out what I wanted, why I wanted it, and learn to express it. I had to go through a lot of introspection and meditation on important subjects. Watching a movie and going rock climbing together is a blast, don't get me wrong, but I can't believe I did so much of that without important topics ever coming up. Waste of money, given that I was paying for all of it. Reach out to your parents today and ask them if they would be willing to suggest a few girls for you to get to know. Now that you know where I'm coming from, let me tell you about the road I took to get here with specific stories from my years of dating. With high hopes for you as … your affectionate uncle, Tio Edwin.

When I was a boy of 14, my father was so ignorant I could hardly stand to have the old man around. But when I got to be 21, I was astonished at how much the old man had learned in 7 years. —Mark Twain

A family tie is like a tree: it can bend, but it cannot break. — African proverb

Dear nephew,

I asked Mary (we'll call her) to be my girlfriend at 14– too young for a serious relationship. I do have beautiful memories from the years we dated, but I am far more glad for the memories I made while dating when I was a college student. Some of the time I spent with Mary made my parents and also my siblings uncomfortable. To be honest, the deep feelings I had for her did not justify how uncomfortable I made them feel. For example, on a couple of occasions I decided to make out with her in public. This is something a child would do, not someone being considerate of others around them. While I was still technically a child, of course I felt my conscience telling me I should stop. It was obvious that we were making my siblings uncomfortable when they walked by. More importantly, I gave up time with my brother, sister, and parents in order to spend it with Mary. This is my biggest regret of starting to date someone seriously so young. Time with family is priceless, and I deeply regret wasting so much time with someone who I would never see after we broke up instead of hanging out with my siblings. After two years of dating, I broke up with Mary. It devastated me. Feeling depressed, I was unable to get out of bed for several days. I felt crushed. Crushed at 16. It might seem silly now, but at the time it was traumatic and soul-draining; the whole ordeal had been momentous for my life. All of this trauma could have been avoided if I had not pretended to be married to my girlfriend at the young age of 14. Years later, my brother would confess that he felt scared when he saw me crying in bed for hours at a time, not able to get up. I had loved this girl. It was the first time in my life I had felt so strongly for someone, and when I broke up with her I physically felt pain and emptiness in my chest. I couldn't stop thinking about her and wondering if I had made a mistake. I started treasuring the music that we had listened to together. I cherished every single gift she had given me. She made me a pillow case that I kept enshrined with other sentimental mementos from her for decades. In fact, I believe it's still in a box in my home somewhere. Your first real love is always the toughest to get over. If I had been older and could have controlled my thoughts and emotions better, I would have realized that we were incompatible in many ways. From our goals, to our religious beliefs, even to where we wanted to live—she was going to live in South America and I was going to stay in North America with my family. It simply wasn't going to work. I should not have jumped into the relationship as if we were married. It was intense, devoted, and—I was convinced—going to end in marriage. How that was going to happen, I had no idea, but that's how I felt. My parents and my siblings were incredibly understanding and supportive. If I could go back, I would make sure to seek their advice and opinions from the beginning. When Mary and I started dating, I simply made the announcement to my family after the decision had been made. Why didn't I ask every member of my family individually before asking her? Why didn't I bring it up during dinner so that we could discuss it collectively? Not only would this have helped me consider many angles to the possibility of dating her, but it would have also been another fear to conquer. Bringing it up this way to my family wouldn't have been easy. Just like we all do on many occasions, I avoided the tough conversations with them. In avoiding the possible awkwardness, I missed out on sharing myself with the people who will always matter the most in my life: my family. Instead of including them in the decision and giving them a front-row seat to what was happening in my inner life, I avoided the topic with them and shut them out during two years of extreme changes in my inner life and thinking process. Mary got the front-row seat on my thoughts and feelings and my family was shut out. All that for some memories of butterflies in my stomach. Some of the memories are beautiful, granted. One time Mary and I met outside in the rain, crying because she was going to leave for an extended period of time. We kissed in the rain, clothes soaking wet while we cried, just like a movie. I know you're not a child anymore, but you have siblings that are younger. Make sure to pass this lesson on to them. Always seek your family's counsel in these decisions, and don't pretend you're married when you're not. While they might be too young to appreciate it now, they'll thank us for it later. It would take years for me to get over that emotional episode, in large part thanks to my second girlfriend, who I'll call Flor. With warm regards from your affectionate uncle, Tio Edwin.

When pure sincerity forms within, it is outwardly realized in other people's hearts. —Lao Tzu

Ever has it been that love knows not its own depth until the hour of separation. —Kahlil Gibran

Dear nephew,

I met the woman I'll call Flor on a trip to Mexico. For me it was a life-changing trip in several ways. We went to help the destitute living in a landfill. The experience opened my eyes to how thankful we should be in this country. As impactful as that was, meeting Flor was definitely the most important event in my romantic life before meeting my wife. We hit it off right away, and she was truly a girl that inspired me to better myself. She came to the U.S. at 13 years of age from Mexico with her family. She showed me respect and always kept herself beautiful and feminine. We also had fun together. The first time she served me food, she was a little offended when I went to serve myself. "I'm your woman, and I'm here to serve you" was her perplexed reaction to me. I was floored and could not believe how lucky I was. We were both 17 years old, but she made me feel like a king. She recognized that I had been hurt by the break up with my previous girlfriend and thought that I had not been as emotionally open with her because of this. She was partly right, but my age was also a factor. Marriage and true commitment were the farthest things from my mind. I was still feeling butterflies every time I saw a pretty girl walk beside me. Emotionally committing to someone— even someone as special and incredible as Flor— was not going to happen. This was especially the case due to the distance between us. She lived in Arizona and I lived in Minnesota. Being the religious woman she is, she often prayed for me and encouraged me to grow in my spiritual life. We dated off and on for about 4 years, but even my freshman year we knew it wasn't working. Fortunately, unlike myself, Flor decided to take action. There were so many changes happening so quickly that I could not make our relationship a priority. Flor knew that our relationship was not progressing. Looking back, I see this was mainly because of all the girls I was meeting and spending time with. The night she broke up with me she did it over the phone. This was a time before cell phones. I had a calling card that I used from a public phone in my dorm entrance. After some conversation, she asked me "Edwin, you don't love me, do you?" She did it in such a gentle, compassionate voice, that I almost answered "yes I do!" My actions had not demonstrated that, however, and I knew it. I also knew that I was stuck in undergraduate school for three more years; I was in no position to offer security in a long-term relationship. Marriage did not even register as an option in my mind. The bottom line was that we had been in a long-term relationship far too long. While I depended on Flor emotionally, I was not becoming attached to her presence because I never had it. Towards the last months of our relationship I had even used the emotional strength I gathered from writing her letters and calling her on the phone in order to diminish the fear I felt when speaking with other girls around me. What did it matter if a girl I ran into while walking to my room rejected an offer to hang out with me? I had all the emotional stability I needed from my girlfriend who lived thousands of miles away. I could feel good about myself again and fill up my emotional tank by calling or writing Flor after a rejection from another girl. While I was emotionally stronger with her in my life, I was in no way getting closer to Flor. This scenario started to happen more and more frequently, although at the time I lacked the emotional sophistication to realize what I was doing. I could sense the situation wasn't right and decided to let the inevitable happen when Flor asked me that question on the pay phone. I did miss her a lot, and for years acknowledged that I was crazy for letting her go. She was definitely the bigger person during the whole relationship. Thanks to her maturity and understanding, we stayed friends for years. Even now I count her as one of the best friends I have ever had. With us both being married, we don't speak as much as we used to, but I will never forget her for as long as I live. If you ever meet a girl like Flor, don't take her for granted. If you find someone like that and you are also at peace with each other (no fights, no awkwardness, no walking on eggshells), then you better explore the possibility of marriage. There is nothing wrong with getting married young. In fact, marrying young is a lot better than waiting and marrying old. If a woman's mere presence in your life gives you an inner strength, peace, and a greater ability to confront the world and whatever it throws at you, put a high value on that woman and don't take her for granted. This emotional security is one of the greatest things a woman can give you. Too bad I was too young and naive to realize it. One can't expect old heads on young shoulders, after all, but you can take advice from older heads, such as... your affectionate uncle, Tio Edwin.

Don't spend time beating a wall, hoping to transform it into a door. —Coco Chanel

In order to make a man or a boy covet a thing, it is only necessary to make the thing difficult to attain. —Mark Twain

Dear Nephew,

My undergraduate years after breaking up with Flor were a mixed bag. I had already started spending time with a wonderful girl I'll call Artemis. Right after the break up, she told me she was glad that I had broken up with Flor. We obviously liked each other but, even though I didn't know it at the time, I felt guilty for spending time with her while I was still dating Flor. The feelings of guilt made me withdraw from her. I would find myself looking for excuses not to date her, even though I was drawn to her. She was a smart woman, though, and had been seeing other people since I hadn't asked for anything official. As soon as I found out, I became jealous. I decided to confront the problem head on and talked with another guy who was making moves on her. It was a rather simple conversation. I asked him "Who likes her more?" After a brief conversation, it was evident this guy was head-over-heels and had no emotional problems being exclusive with her. We both agreed it was obvious he should pursue a relationship with her. Today, they are married and have three children! While we rarely interact on social media, I was very happy when I found them and joked with the guy that he needed to thank me! That is one conversation I'm glad I had. In fact, I've confronted several men who were interested in the same woman I was, and every time it has always turned out well. Our respect for each other always grew, and it quickly turned hurtful situations into ones that were resolved quickly. Transparency and honesty are the antidote to hurt feelings and drama. The only caveat would be that honesty needs to be communicated with respect and tactfulness. The point isn't to lash out, but rather to communicate what your desires are, learn about the other person's desires, and see if there is a win/win going forward. If this is kept in mind every step of the way, much unnecessary drama and hurt can be avoided. I dated several women during my undergraduate years following this event, but nothing serious. I even met several girls through online sites. One in particular had put up gorgeous pictures of herself. I traveled all the way to Humbolt Park in Chicago to meet her at her college, but upon meeting her I was so disappointed I couldn't hide it. She was not nearly as attractive and in shape as her pictures showed. After that disappointment, I didn't try online dating again for several years. I did know an older woman I'll call Karma who I was very interested in. I regret that I never expressed this to her. She was about 9 years older than me and I felt like I didn't have anything to give her. This, along with a serious "friend zoning" that happened, and our vibe was just not romantic. Many times she would call me at 5am and tell me to get up because we were going to get breakfast together. It was an awesome friendship with a beautiful woman inside and out, and I appreciated every minute of it. I knew her for years without expressing my feelings. What a shame, especially considering how easy it is to move a relationship away from the "friend zone." The steps are these:

1. Let her know what she means to you IN PERSON, without any joking.
2. Tell her what you want from her and wait for her response.
3. If she can't reciprocate, say you can be friends, but things will be different for a while.

That's it. There's no mystery to it. If you find yourself in the friend zone and can't figure out what to do, just go through these steps with her the next time you are alone and able to talk. You will not regret it, whichever way the relationship develops. If you are afraid that you might not be able to say everything you want, there's nothing wrong with writing it down. However, make sure to read it to her IN PERSON, not just send it to her through texts or online. Important conversations must be had in person. If you guys live in different continents, then don't have the conversation until you are able to do it in person. I had my share of long distance relationships and, trust me, you want to spend plenty of time in person before you ask for a deeper level of commitment anyway. There's a saying in Spanish: "Amor de lejos, felices los cuatro." I put myself in that long-distance situation for far too long, and the saying turned out true for me. Don't put yourself in that same situation. Know what you want, always communicate it along the way, and don't be afraid to change course when you don't know what you want. Confusion and uncertainty also need to be communicated. With warm regards from your affectionate Uncle, Tio Edwin.

God is a comedian playing to an audience that is too afraid to laugh. —Voltaire

Just remain in the center, watching. Then forget that you are there. —Lao Tzu

Dear nephew,

Amitra was a wonderful girl from Saudi Arabia. I immediately thought she was really interesting and I began taking Arabic lessons from her on a regular basis. We also began to frequent the same social circles. I was intrigued by her personal and family story, but more than that she was just fun to be around. She had an easy smile, would always contribute to the conversation, and every now and then would initiate something to do. She gave off the vibe of being one of the boys most of the time, but I was so intrigued by her demeanor and the easy-going dynamic she inspired in me and others around her that I began to really crave her presence. As soon as I noticed that, I realized that I had a huge crush on her. I couldn't believe it. I had always thought that people who got crushes they couldn't articulate were silly. Having gone through the phase of approaching women that intimidated me, I didn't think a girl could intimidate me like this. Here I was feeling intimidated, however, not because she was completely unapproachable, but quite the opposite. We would sit and have really fun banter, I would love having it, and then be afraid of how attracted I was feeling to her. At one point we were hanging out at the communal kitchen of the dorm room with a couple of friends. One guy had an incredible amount of phlegm and had to spit it out. He went to the sink and slowly let it roll down his tongue. Amitra, instead of being grossed out, said, "Yeah. Just let it roll down slowly," while cracking up at him. She turned a disgusting situation into one that made her look so chill, and relaxed, and fun, and.... attractive! I wanted to tell her, but how does one turn a situation like that into one that is attractive to you? I didn't have the vocabulary or self-consciousness to explain why I was attracted to her, so I just stayed quiet about it. The more I stayed quiet, the more intimidated I got. I was hoping that she might become interested in me, but she was a young woman who had lived a lot: she had lived in three different continents, had to help her family survive some tough times, and had seen a lot. I wasn't doing much to improve my life either, so how could I hope for someone like her to become interested in me? Like most undergraduate men, I went to classes and, after finishing homework, hung out with friends. I wasn't working on a business. I wasn't making plans to travel. I wasn't even contemplating the things I was learning in classes so that at least I could discuss interesting subjects with her. Whenever we got together, it was just small talk and banter about what friends were doing. I would ask her personal questions about her family and her past, but that was about it. I was thoroughly friend-zoned in her mind. People describe that now as giving her too much "value" while not valuing myself enough. Perhaps. The bottom line is that I was not improving my own life while getting completely immersed in the friend zone. Even though I admired this woman, I should have focused on learning from her as much as I could in order to keep improving myself. When I simply couldn't take it anymore, instead of going up to her and speaking in person, I decided to give her a gift with a written note describing my feelings. This move would not have helped me get out of the friend zone but would instead help solidify that position beyond repair. If I had spoken to her in person clearly describing my feelings, what I wanted, and what would happen if we couldn't take my feelings into consideration, at least there would have been a chance we could've had a romantic relationship. I would have been rocking the boat confidently and given her a chance to consider it seriously. I didn't even give her the gift personally, instead just left it at her door. She called me when she found it and said thank you, but that we were friends and she wasn't interested. "Don't worry, you'll find your Amitra someday," was one of the last things she told me in that conversation. I had not only failed to take the situation by the horns, even in that phone call, I let her completely dictate how the conversation would proceed. I thanked her for her kindness and said we could still be friends, although we never got close. We would be friendly, but the frequent Arabic lessons fizzled out. Our social circles became separate and we simply moved on. I should have made a decision in which direction I wanted to take the relationship, told her in person, and given us a couple of possibilities on how to proceed once I heard her response, instead of being paralyzed by fear. If you are decisive, even being in the friend zone shouldn't be a problem. Warm regards from your affectionate uncle, Tio Edwin.

If we really want to love, we must learn how to forgive. —*Saint Teresa of Calcutta,*
The longer we dwell on our misfortunes, the greater is their power to harm us. —*Voltaire*

Dear nephew,

I thought I wasn't good enough to play in the wind ensemble of my undergraduate school, but they needed a saxophone, so I was in. The highlight became seeing an oboe player I'll call Ana. She was a light blonde with a skinny body, a beautiful face, and was always friendly to me. I sat a few rows behind her during class, and a few times she looked back at me with a smile and prolonged eye contact that I still remember to this day.We ended up eating together a few times, and I walked her to her dorm room whenever I could. I was becoming quite fond of Ana after spending time together. I loved hearing her play her oboe. The oboe has a hauntingly beautiful sound. Played by such a beautiful woman, the experience was magical. I liked talking to Ana while she cut her oboe reeds. The double-reed of the oboe has to be cut and shaped by the player. This is done with a sharp knife that looks quite ominous. Such a beautiful girl holding that knife—her forearm and hand muscles straining— while looking up at me smiling was a surprisingly attractive scene. The walk back to Ana's dorm room was about 15 minutes. During this day's walk, I had been wanting to tell her how I felt. We reached her dorm and I said goodbye as usual without saying anything. I felt defeated as I walked away from her door. Suddenly, I felt a surge of courage. I turned around and decided to go knock on her door. She opened the door with her usual bright, beautiful smile. I told her she was beautiful and I really enjoyed spending time with her. Would she like to go out on a date with me? She kept the same smile she first greeted me with. After listening to me, she said, "Oh, you thought that I liked you?" Her tone was such that she might as well have said, "Oh, you thought that I could like you?" Her unflinching facial expression was chilling. She seemed oblivious that I could have hurt feelings. My heart sank. "No, of course not. I just thought that since... we had been spending so much time together... no, of course you don't like me. Sorry to bother. See you later." Immediately after saying this, she said "Ok, bye!" with the same unflinching smile. Humiliated, I started my walk. I noticed the beautiful spring flowers that lavishly decorated the trees, a common spring site in college settings. They were small and pink and had a subtle aroma that followed me everywhere. It was lovely. As I walked back to my dorm, I wondered if I had misread the situation. This last interaction put the previous months of interaction into perspective. My mind went back to all her questions about where I was from. Slowly it dawned on me that in her mind I was her multicultural buddy. It's important for us to recognize that the majority of the world is brown or black. White skin is an adaptation for extremely cold climates so people don't die of vitamin D deficiency. Naturally, white women are seen as exotic around the world, given that there are so few of them. Since America exports its movies and culture (and white people have been the majority in this country), white women have been further elevated as desirable around the world.

Because of this, it's easy for us to view white women with romantic potential. Now picture the cultural portrayal of short, minority men such as myself. We are comic relief, at best. I assumed she wanted to know me personally; silly me. I remained cordial, but I never walked her to her dorm again. She never stopped addressing me in the exact same manner, with the exact same smile and facial expressions. I knew that it was a smile directed towards my race and skin color. She was being friendly towards a race, instead of an individual. You'll notice that North American liberal women in particular will exhibit this tendency. They will see you as a representative of a group, not as an individual with feelings. It won't dawn on them that you have just as deep, as rich, and as complicated an inner life as they do. Given that I am 5-foot nothing, it was much easier for her to put me in this category without realizing it. She was taller than me, after all. Especially in northern areas of the U.S., height has an abnormally important place in determining a man's attractiveness. Thankfully you are taller than I am. I hope you will avoid being placed in the multicultural buddy zone, which is several notches below the dreaded friend zone. We have white people in our family, making it much easier to see skin color as just another aspect of an individual, not their entire self. Sadly, not everybody grows up with this advantage. I would have similar experiences after this one. It would take years for me to stop putting up walls against white people— particularly white women—that came into my life. Prejudice is not the cure for prejudice. With warm regards from your affectionate uncle, Tio Edwin.

One frequently only finds out how really beautiful a beautiful woman is after considerable acquaintance with her. —Mark Twain

We are like sculptors, constantly carving out of others the image we long for, need, love or desire, often against reality, against their benefit, and always, in the end, a disappointment, because it does not fit them. —Anais Nin

Dear Nephew,

My little sister Maried warned me, but I didn't listen. It was May 26, 2001, when I met the most beautiful girl in the world. I was traveling in Europe with a school choir when I decided to visit some friends in Austria. My friends met me at a train station about 2 hours from where I was staying. Meeting their families was great, but the highlight of my trip was meeting Zahar. When the door opened, I was awestruck. She had dark-mocha skin, a full figure, tight jeans, a blouse that showed her entire navel, and messy hair scrunched on top of her head with small flecks of black hair cascading down randomly over her face and down to her shoulders. I was completely mesmerized by her and unable to hide it. She became quite coy as we walked in and I sat next to her on the floor. She noticed that I was completely taken by her and put a red hibiscus flower in her hair while smiling at me. It was surreal. She didn't speak English, so we tried to communicate the best we could. Others stepped in and tried to be interpreters. She was a Persian girl who had lived in Austria most of her life. I took down her email address and promised her I was going to keep in touch. I came back home determined to visit her the following summer and started working odd jobs to save enough to travel. A few times she sent pictures, but she would never write much. It was obvious she was not interested in learning English, while I didn't have time to learn German. My family was amused to see me in love like this; everyone, except my little sister who seemed skeptical. What was this Zahar telling me about herself? What did I know about her? All I knew was that she was the most beautiful girl in the world! My sister grew so frustrated with me that she told me, "I bet she really stinks up a room when she farts." A teenage sister's frustration with her brother for assuming a girl is an angel and not a real human being. Throughout the school year I socialized with other people, but in the back of my mind, Zahar was always present. Her beauty and flirtatiousness had made such an impression that I couldn't shake it. A girl at school started pursuing me quite directly that year, but I had to wait and see for myself what the next summer would bring when I went back to spend time with the most beautiful girl in the world. The time finally came. My parents were quite worried for me and told me to make sure to come back. This would not be the last time they would tell me not to get married in Europe. I was going to stay with my friend's boyfriend, Alex. His family's house was less than an hour from Vienna, which was convenient. When I arrived, Alex picked me up. We were having a blast, but I was anxious to see Zahar. I had emailed her and told her I was coming back, but the first two days there I had not been able to see her. Finally, I had Alex just drive me to her house. I called her and she said she would be happy to see me in her broken English. When I got there, something was off. Her mother came out to entertain me. I got straight to the point. I told the woman I thought her daughter was beautiful and I wanted to spend time with her. Her mother laughed a little and, while striking a pose like a model, said Zahar was beautiful, just like her mother. I had just spent thousands of dollars to fly over and see this girl. Where was she? I politely asked if she was home. She was. Her mother walked me back to her room and I finally greeted her. We sat down on her bed and tried chatting. She seemed preoccupied with dressing up. She was heading to work soon. I asked her where she worked, but she didn't want to tell me. I was taken aback. I wasn't meaning to pry, just wanted to make small talk and get to know her. We headed out to the living room where Alex helped in translating. I started wondering what line of work she had gotten herself into. I asked Alex if he knew what she did, but he said he didn't and she didn't want to say. Was she a high-end escort? Zahar told Alex she was very sorry that she had to leave. I left their apartment embarrassed and with my heart broken. Alex consoled me by telling me that in the year I had been away, things had changed a lot in their friend group. They didn't get along anymore and nobody had seen Zahar for a while. He didn't know exactly what she did, but he just wouldn't recommend me pursuing her. That was the last time I saw Zahar. I emailed a few more times after that, but we simply stopped communicating. I did get to spend the rest of the time exploring Austria, which was definitely not a waste of time. The whole thing had been a hugely embarrassing episode, especially when I had to explain how it went to my family back home. I should have listened to my little sister. Giving more weight to my family's opinions seems to be a theme in these letters, doesn't it? With warm regards from your affectionate uncle, Tio Edwin.

To get lost is to learn the way. —African proverb

To attain knowledge, add things every day. To attain wisdom, remove things every day.
—Lao Tzu

Dear Nephew,

    I started graduate school near St. Louis on a clean slate. It was exciting to be in a new city at 21. Still very young, I easily related to the undergraduate students around me, and my social life became full very quickly. I'm glad for that. Theresa was a dirty-blond, fabulously energetic dance student who lived in the moment and made me see magic everywhere. We would take car rides on a whim. She would be fascinated by my opinions, and I made her feel special. On one occasion, we snuck into the fabulous Fox Theater, downtown St. Louis, and were blown away by the beauty. We relished that nobody kicked us out! We admired the gold ornaments and massive chandelier for what seemed like half an hour before we snuck back out. On one occasion we entered a dance studio alone. After dancing together, she told me I should let go of my body, bounce around, and forget about my inhibitions; after a while, I stopped caring that I looked ridiculous. It was wonderful, and I was head-over-heels in a matter of weeks. However, this feeling turned into obsession as quickly as it developed. The problem was that Theresa would give me her wonderful, undivided attention for days at a time, and then all of a sudden would not return my phone calls for a week. I didn't realize what was happening or why this "hot/cold" approach towards me made me desperate to see her.

It's basic psychology and one that every kindergartener knows instinctively, but at the time I was so inside of the situation that I couldn't see why my feelings had intensified so quickly. I finally confronted her and she told me the reason for her absences. Theresa could not be exclusive with me because she had been seeing somebody else for some time. Even though she did not love him, she felt guilty and didn't want to break up with him. Still thinking that dating more than one person at a time was a horrible thing (and thus feeling terrible and cheated on) I was devastated. This is probably the only time in my adult life I truly felt depressed, to the point of not being able to get out of bed. Now I know that the interaction I was having with her is called "Random Interval Reward System." RIRS is the reason why some people become addicted to gambling. Rewards are random, with different time intervals between them, and it leaves the person looking for that reward more and more. Theresa didn't know she was doing this to me, but her random rewards for me were of time, affection, excitement, etc. The more time went by, the more I craved the rewards of spending time with her. We were on the brink of becoming physical a few times, but just as our bodies came closer and our hands held the other, she would change the subject and disappear for the night. I didn't know what was happening at the time, but it led me to become increasingly needy and sad when I couldn't have her company. My mother was a huge help at this time and told me to go church hoping. I was to go find a church with the largest number of young people, become part of it, and start befriending others. I had become isolated with my obsession with Theresa—socializing was just what I needed. That first Sunday I felt like I couldn't carry a decent conversation with anybody, but having my mother's explicit instructions of what to do gave me strength. I can't express how glad I am that my mother pushed me to do that. I met a really wonderful crew of people I just loved to spend time with. One guy in particular gave me great memories. While no longer in touch, I will never forget the light-hearted way Jake brought happiness to others. One time he got on one knee and proposed to a total stranger in a restaurant just for our amusement. With new friends, I had strength to act. I confronted the guy that Theresa had been seeing. He was not good for her, but I was tired of the emotional turmoil. I told Theresa I never wanted to speak with her again. I was cruel, ignoring her in public when she said hello, even in front of others. I ignored her for 9 months while secretly keeping tabs on where she was. I had even memorized her license plate in case I came across her car, like some stalker. That time apart was enough for me to be able to emotionally move on. I'm glad I decisively stopped that negative cycle. When we began talking again, she expressed how my firm response led her to respect me more. Don't be afraid to separate yourself from someone if you are miserable. A sincere and rewarding friendship is possible even after having romantic feelings. We met years later with our spouses at one of her dance performances. It was a wonderful meeting. Theresa offers an emotional ocean for her husband to explore. It's a beautiful thing to see. With warm regards from your affectionate uncle, Tio Edwin.

Do not look back when leaving. Pythagoras

Never argue with a fool. Onlookers may not be able to tell the difference. —*Mark Twain,*

Dear nephew,

I met a girl I'll call Janey during the time I was ignoring Theresa in the new Bible study I'd found. She was from a white-African family from Central Africa. I was fascinated by their story and ended up unthinkingly placing her in the friend zone. She was quite a bit taller than me and had a really fun personality with a nice, curvy body. I never suspected she could become interested in me. This girl was beautiful, with a very interesting family and cultural history, but she was surrounded by people and engaged in activities that would've dragged my life down. It would take a few months for another woman in the group to approach me and tell me Janey might be falling in love with me. At first I didn't believe it. I was also annoyed that her confidence would be betrayed like that—perhaps Janey didn't want me to know she had a crush on me. I was determined to not let that get in the way of our friendship. If Janey felt something for me, she would have to let me know personally before I assumed I should not hang out with her. I made sure to talk with her normally and say yes if she invited me to do anything. Just being open to her friendship would end up causing the death-nail of the relationship, however. We began to take frequent expeditions around town and into the city in her car, and it was usually a great time. The more I got to know her, however, the more concerned I became for her. She was taking a few drugs that, besides being illegal, could end up affecting her health. I also felt her social life was not filled with the best people. On one occasion, she took me to meet one of her friends who was a gay man. This is almost a decade before the 2015 Supreme Court decision to legalize gay marriage, so being gay was still seen as something counter cultural and risqué. Naturally as hip young people we were both very attracted to seeing ourselves as cool and risqué, so we were looking forward to hanging out. We ended up having a good time, full of laughter and witty banter, but before we left the guy joked that there's no way he would ever be attracted to breasts—as if being a gay man meant he couldn't recognize the beauty in of woman's body. Right after this statement, however, he began to fondle Janey's breasts, at which point she made an exaggerated gesture of surprise. After a few chuckles, he slapped her breast in an upward motion, making her breasts bounce up in an abnormal fashion as she continued laughing with mock surprise, mouth gaping open. The conversation continued for a few brief moments before we had to leave. It happened very quickly, but something about that last interaction felt disrespectful, not just to Janey, but also to me. I had just met this guy. Why was he fondling my friend's breast right in front of me? Also, why had she not even flinched? Was this a common occurrence? She had obviously wanted me to meet her friends to show how exciting they were and for me to become more interested in her, but having another man fondle your breasts is not the best way to have a guy become interested in you. The whole thing had just been weird and off-putting, but I rolled with it. Janey was relying on drugs to cope with every-day stressors. I began to tell her she should stop taking them… it just wasn't good for her. Insisting it wasn't a big deal and I just shouldn't worry about it, this became an argument that we started having frequently. Finally, I'd had enough. I insisted that a good friend would not let her do this to herself. I called the cops and asked them what could be done to stop her. There wasn't much they could do, but that phone call would end up being enough. I told her that I called the cops and that I would tell them exactly who she was if she didn't stop. She was livid with me. This would end up being the last private conversation we would ever have. I wouldn't speak with her again, even though we were in the same social circle. When I left town the following year, we completely lost touch with each other. I'm grateful I finally did the right thing and insisted, for her own good, that she stop doing drugs. If circumstances had been different, she could've easily gotten me into experimenting with drugs myself. The relationship would've been one full of dysfunction, awkwardness, and unnecessary risk taking. I'm glad I did the right thing and did not tolerate too much of that around me. Most times, just doing what you know to be the right thing will drive away the wrong people from your life and save you a lot of heartache, time, and trouble. If you tell the truth as you see it, a lot of problems will end up working themselves out without having to put much thought into them. To this day, I hope she has her life together and wish Janey the best, but

I'm glad I never made an emotional commitment. Her never speaking with me again became an afterthought. In fact, I felt bad for her about it. She missed out on having me as a friend in her life. With warm regards from your affectionate uncle, Tio Edwin.

Sincerity cannot be ridiculous and always deserves respect. —
Charlotte Bronte

Life without love is no life at all. —*Leonardo da Vinci*

Dear Nephew,

While studying for my first Masters degree, I
noticed one guy in particular acting a little differently
around me. I'll call him Piñero. He would stand a little too
close, give me a little too much attention, and laugh a little
too enthusiastically when I spoke. I liked him and chalked
it up to social awkwardness. Once while we were talking in
a group, he stood close to me, touched my shirt just beside
my shoulder, and said, "I really like your shirt." He
maintained contact for too long, and I felt sorry for him.
"Poor guy," I thought to myself. "He doesn't know that
men don't do that in this culture." It happened again during
a music recital. While sitting in an empty row, Piñero
walked in, said hello, and jumped on the seat right next to
me. Once again, I thought, "Poor guy. He doesn't know
men usually leave a seat between each other." After some
small talk, he mentioned again how he liked my clothing;
this time my pants. However, he proceeded to place his
right index finger on my left thigh a couple of inches above
my knee. "This poor guy. I'm gonna have to tell him
somehow that he doesn't know how to interact with men."
The recital ended, but before the night was done, a female
friend of mine approached me. "Edwin, you do know that
Piñero is gay, right?" "What?! No, I hadn't even thought

about it." "Yeah, he really likes you." That's what was going on! When girls fell in my "friend zone" I was usually clueless about these things, so there's no way I was going to consider the possibility of him flirting with me. I didn't want to hurt his feelings, so I treated him like any girl I was trying to discourage romantically: I didn't talk much to him, if he approached me I was cordial but didn't linger, and I made sure to hang out with other people if I knew we were going to be at the same event. A few months of this and everything was cool again. I'm a straight, classical pianist and have done plenty of music theater and other artistic endeavors. The arts attract extroverts willing to experiment, so I was constantly surrounded by men and women of all persuasions. That wasn't the only time I dealt with same sex attraction in my life by any means. There was even a time where I questioned my own sexuality. That didn't make me special, it made me human. This LGBTQ+ obsession currently engulfing every aspect of our culture is baffling and, frankly, ridiculous. Any human being who mainly identifies with whatever arouses them sexually has childishly and pathetically reduced their humanity. Sex is great, but it's only a part of relationships, which of themselves are just an aspect of a whole person. In the West, there is so little pride in our culture that this is one way to regain some sense of group identity. This is especially true in the U.S., the most individualistic country in the world. So many families are broken and so many have no connection to their ancestors or cultural heritage that people resort to inventing nonsense about belonging to a group based on what arouses them sexually. It's ridiculous and laughable on its face. I've met plenty of Americans who outright say they have no culture. I guess if you're completely unaware of your heritage, language, family lineage, or cultural place in history, you might as well take pride in whatever turns you on. It's an extension of those pubescent years of adolescence where your sexuality took up a large part of your mental energy. Remember those? You probably grew out of it by the time you hit 16 or 17 and had some real-world problems to worry about. The LGBT movement is "failure to launch" using sexuality as an emotional anchor. That little LGBT acronym has been accruing letters every other year or so. Pretty soon you'll have grown adults identifying with those who get turned on by sounds, or the color purple, or kids cartoons. Wait, that first one is an actual thing. Honestly, you're living in times that are beyond parody. If you should ever be tempted to wrestle with your sexuality, given the ridiculous cultural obsession all around us, just remember that you marry one person, not an entire sex, gender, or identity. There are more than 7 billion people on this earth, each with an entirely different sexuality. The problem with that ridiculous acronym is that it should be 7 billion letters long if it were to realistically reflect the full diversity of sexualities in this world. Your own sexuality will change through time. When you find your wife, you'll grow and change together. I have technically nothing against polygamy, but there is such a depth of growth and change when you marry one woman, I pity men with more than one wife. Married people have much more sex than single people, by the way. You're living in the generation that has the least amount of sex in recorded history—probably in world history. Don't let that be you. Find a good woman, love her, marry her, and bang her brains out as often as you can. You aren't making love to an entire sex in a political gesture, you're making love to one person you're growing with and learning to love. With warm regards from your affectionate uncle, Tio Edwin.

I prefer you make mistakes in kindness than work miracles in unkindness. —*Saint Teresa of Calcutta*

It is a naive sort of feminism that insists that women prove their ability to do all the things that men do. This is a distortion and a travesty. Men have never sought to prove that they can do all the things women do. Why subject women to purely masculine criteria? ... To be a woman is not to be a man. To be married is not to be single - which may mean not to have a career. To marry this man is not to marry all the others. A choice is a limitation.
—*Elisabeth Elliot*

Dear Nephew,

Mandy was a trumpet player I became interested in while I was ignoring Theresa. As often as I could, I would leave her a piece of candy at her instrument locker. I had asked her to go out with me, but she was in the middle of a breakup. For months I persisted in asking her out. You'll notice that the females who reject you kindly will be the ones that you become interested in the most. I thought I could be good to her. Unfortunately, I did not live up to my standards. I came to regret my actions towards her immensely. We got along great for our entire relationship. She really respected me and looked up to me. Mandy was so kind and gentle that, for some reason, I began to think that perhaps she just wasn't "street smart" or savvy enough. We dated for almost a year before I broke up with her because of this moronic attitude I developed. I thought I was more sophisticated than her and needed someone more exciting. Someone who would push back on me when I said something dumb instead of being so understanding and gentle. She had the habit of turning negative interactions into peaceful ones. If I got lost while traveling somewhere, instead of getting annoyed at me she would smile and say that at least we got to spend extra time in the car together. Believe it or not, little interactions like that struck me as unsophisticated. I can't believe how stupid I was being. This is an attitude that you will see everywhere in academia. Constantly surrounded by people who specialize in different aspects of their discipline and display superior attitudes— many actually are intellectually superior to you — can start to rub off and make you feel superior to others in all aspects of life, not just in your specific area of specialization. This is a huge mistake I hope you never fall into. I consider my attitude towards Mandy one of the worst mistakes I ever made. At the end of our relationship I allowed myself to treat her with a bit of disdain. This is unacceptable behavior from a man to a woman. A few years after breaking up I realized how stupid I'd been. One evening while thinking about her, I looked and looked for her on a social network. After a long time, I found her. I had come to realize how important it was for me to find a woman who was gentle, kind, and considerate. Finding Mandy online was an emotional moment. She had married someone else and had several children with him. As soon as I saw the pictures I began crying at my computer. It suddenly hit me how gentle she had been with me, how much she had looked up to me, and how little I had valued her. After meeting so many Americans that consider traditionally feminine attributes a weakness, I was glad to see she married a gentleman from an African country. I hoped this man would appreciate her gentleness and femininity. Many think this is becoming a rarity in the West, myself included. While there are many laudable aspects of American dating life, the negative seem to increasingly outweigh the good. The complete lack of awareness of other ways of courting and marrying is one of them, but certainly not the worst. There seems to be a peculiar inability to account for differences between the sexes here. The traditionally feminine virtues— such as beauty, compassion, grace, gentleness— seem to be regarded as less important than the traditionally masculine virtues of strength, courage, mastery, and honor. Think of how many women feel like it would be a waste of time to primarily be a mother instead of following their career dreams. By the time I was dating Mandy, I had internalized the feeling that these feminine virtues were useless hindrances. While we can't pursue someone only because they are a "girly girl," I hope you will never dismiss someone from your life simply because they are traditionally feminine. This has got to be one of the most absurd places in relationships between the sexes that any culture has reached: a culture that puts women down for being feminine. Let's hope the pendulum swings to a more balanced place soon enough. In your personal life, you will not regret looking for a gentle, feminine spirit in a woman. The complementary aspects between the sexes are common sense and have been taught in all faith traditions throughout all human history. Romantic relationships are the norm, not the exception, and we would be wise to learn from thousands of years of experimentation and accumulation of knowledge. We didn't suddenly become better humans because Tinder came along. Be masculine, but look for and cherish the feminine. With warm regards from your affectionate uncle, Tio Edwin.

A good traveler has no fixed plan, and is not intent on arriving.
—Lao Tzu

Pursue what catches your heart, not what catches your eyes. —
Roy T. Bennett

Dear Nephew,

Be careful what you wish for. The same month I broke up with Mandy, I met a girl I'll call Bunny. I was at a salsa dance party in St. Louis when I saw this angel on the other side of a crowded room. She had red, voluminous hair down to the middle of her back. Her gorgeous face with mischievous eyes smiled in my direction. She was the type of girl that makes men nervous to breathe. Being 5'-nothing, I wasn't expecting attention from her. She stood about 5'9" tall. Her figure was beautiful. She had long legs, beautiful arms and a long, delicate neck. I referred to her as "Jessica Rabbit" to my friends due to her figure and sex appeal. I was transfixed. After one quick dance, I mentioned how beautiful I thought she was. She thanked me for the compliment and in a low, airy voice told me "it's your job to see if you can get my number tonight." She walked away from me in a way that gave me arrhythmic palpitations. I was over the moon. We went out about a week later. I invited her to a musical in the same Fox Theater that Theresa and I had snuck into the year before. She wore an incredible Indian Sari that showed her mi section, along with a metal arm-band that coiled around her left bicep. Her shoulders were only partially covered and her hair was down. I'd never been stunned into silence by a girl's beauty like this. After sitting down on the left hand side of the balcony seats and some conversation, she asked how old I thought she was. An awful feeling in my stomach ensued immediately. I hadn't even considered her age. "Wait, you're not 13 or something are you?!" I asked, trying not to seem scared but failing miserably. After a charming laugh, she said "I'm 17," in her airy, alto voice. I was so relieved. I was 21— a four-year difference. As a Christian I was not planning on sleeping with this girl anyway. I gave a sigh of relief. I said I didn't care, she was the most beautiful woman I'd ever seen. We agreed to meet again. She was weeks away from turning 18 and as soon as the day came I asked her to be my girlfriend. We had spent some time together already (walking in parks, reading books, etc.) and I was absolutely taken with her. I even arranged for her to meet the crew of guys I hung with. She handled herself beautifully with them. Andrew, who was the playboy-type in the group, even asked her some uncomfortable, suggestive questions meant to intimidate and tease her. She took it all in stride and retorted with some of her own witty banter. It was amazing. The guys were so impressed that right after the date they called me and left the message: "Alright guys... all together. 1, 2, 3... Well done Edwin!!" I had never felt so much respect from other men for being with a woman. She was also fluent in Spanish. I soon met her family at her house. We had a lovely meal together with her father and younger sister. I got along quite well with her father, someone who had been through a lot and was raising his daughters alone. I respected him, and we ended up exchanging letters. I also thought her sister was fun and we got along. More importantly, every single time I met with Bunny I was more attracted to her. She had an artistic, adventurous temperament that was also a bit rebellious. On one occasion we were in the car and I thought I would stop for fast food. She said in a concerned tone, "I can't go in there Edwin! That place isn't for white people. Only black people go in there!" I couldn't believe what I was hearing. I insisted she walk in with me. She was right. There were no white faces in the entire restaurant. Everybody turned to look at her as we walked in. It suddenly got very quiet and the tension was palpable. It was like something out of a movie, but I ordered our chicken and ate it in peace. We came out with a story to tell after going through that discomfort. How could this relationship not last? I dreamed that it would last for years. I even started to make plans for a marriage proposal. Unfortunately, things started to turn negative only in a matter of months. Our first argument came about because we disagreed about whether children should be allowed to experiment with drugs. I regret that our discussions got so serious so quickly. Why in the world were we talking about having children before I knew the first thing about her? In this relationship I made the unfortunate mistake of allowing myself to get carried away by the moment, rather than leading us through the myriad of options we had in getting to know each other. I will tell you about the unfortunate end of this relationship in the next letter. With warm regards from your affectionate uncle, Tio Edwin.

Charm is deceitful, and beauty is vain, But a woman who fears the Lord, she shall be praised. —Proverbs 31:30

One frequently only finds out how really beautiful a beautiful woman is after considerable acquaintance with her. —Mark Twain

Dear Nephew,

Bunny and I should have been having fun together! True to form, I had to fall into a quasi-marriage. After some tortured discussions about children, we agreed to disagree. Small little issues turned into epic fights between us after exploring the depths of this initial topic, however. She wasn't used to men disagreeing. The situation that escalated our break up happened during a halloween-themed date I planned. I decorated things in black to watch a scary movie in my apartment. I waited for her to show up, but she finally arrived almost an hour late. Not someone to let things like that bother me, I didn't even ask her why she had been late as I saw her arrive. I got into my "Igor" voice to welcome her into the creepy castle (along with a black-cat pillow I had placed on the futon). She laughed and, after a brief apology for being so late, we settled in. We didn't finish the movie before we began kissing and Bunny got on top of me. I should've stopped it before it started but I gently lifted her body away from mine and told her "we should probably cool it" before we both collapsed back, movie still playing in the background. The experience for me had been magical. At first she seemed happy too, but almost immediately she began to get upset. After a few moments of silence, she wanted to leave and the night ended abruptly. What had gone wrong? I couldn't make it out. The next conversation was a huge blow up on the phone. She felt bad that I wanted to stop being so physical with her. "I want you to want to kiss me!" she said loudly. I explained that of course I wanted her. I felt it was immoral to be so physical so quickly. The conversation blew up to a point where she wanted nothing to do with me. The whole conversation was a shock to me. After a couple of days we got together again, but it didn't last long. The last time we communicated was through email. She mentioned a couple of ways in which I was being unreasonable with her and how she needed to feel wanted. I told her that after getting her "foreigner fix," she was done with me. It was all very passionate, very serious, and very intense. In her last email, she wrote "put a fork in it!" I had to ask my friend Jake what that meant, and he told me she broke up with me. He was one of the guys in the crew that had called and yelled "well done!" Her father and I exchanged a couple of letters after we broke up. He gave me suggestions on how I might patch things up with her and asked me to be patient. It was a little late, however, as I was finishing my first master's degree and leaving the city. That summer I moved to Nashville where I interned for a record company. I was a little over 4 hours away, and I took that highway through St. Louis often to visit friends and family. Every single time I drove through, I wanted to stop and see Bunny. Several times I even parked at her house, but I could not get myself to go up to the door. I was sure she was on to the next man. She was so gorgeous, I couldn't imagine anybody saying no to her. We did briefly meet for her to return a book that I had lent her. The magic was gone, however. She no longer spoke to me the same way, looked at me the same way, or walked away from me the same way. I missed her for years, and every time I drove through St. Louis, I would play "her song" in my car. Years later while living in Fargo, I received a random phone call from her. She married a man 25 years older than her. After 3 children, her marriage was on the rocks. She called me and sincerely asked me why I hadn't been more patient. She wished she had not been so hasty with me. I was grateful for her comments. "It had just been a different stage in life," I explained, "and we were both so young." We were both passionate people; fire that burns hot usually burns quickly. I contemplated asking her to get back together, but one of my rules is that I will avoid raising another man's children. She had three. After a few conversations and letters, we agreed to stop communicating because she was still married; it was becoming inappropriate. While we did the right thing, this was the first time I had a romantic conversation with a married woman. I saw through social media some months later that she had gotten a divorce. I do hope for the best that life has to offer her. She gave me some beautiful memories. Many times you will have to offend someone in order to avoid temptation. Knowing what you want will help you avoid what you don't want. Don't just learn to hate bad things; it's better to foster a love for good things. To this day I'm glad I stopped the physical aspect of that relationship as it might have led to a pregnancy. I would have done my duty, of course, but I would have been forced to be with someone that was not compatible with me at the time. Gut feelings and conscience are important too. Warm regards from your affectionate uncle, Tio Edwin.

If you don't let your husband drink beer with men, he will start drinking champagne with women. —Ayn Rand

There is more hunger in the world for love and appreciation than for bread. —Saint Teresa of Calcutta

Dear Nephew,

The moment I learned not to judge others for falling into temptation was my first encounter with a prostitute. I went against the advice of my mother and moved to Nashville during the summer of 2005 working for a music publishing company and a separate talent agency. It was exciting because Dolly Parton recorded in that building. I was not going to be paid much, so I had to live in the cheapest place I could find, which wasn't in the best neighborhood. I was a single guy and going to be working all day anyway, so I would just go home to sleep. The whole experience was a ton of work, but very rewarding. I would get hundreds of demo CDs each week from aspiring artists. If I found anything promising, I was to kick it up for the boss to consider. There was so much to listen to on top of all my other duties, that each group or artist had 10 seconds to catch my attention before I took out the CD and put in the next one. I also found a good Hispanic church. Most of my friends were undocumented immigrants and we had plans of rooming together, although I left before that could happen. There were a few times when they even helped me with food since I hardly had any income. I had no social media so I haven't kept in touch, but I do remember them fondly and often wonder where life has taken them. I hope we meet again some day. One morning I was waiting at the gas station for an open spot when I noticed one of the three women who always stood at a nearby corner approaching me. She was obviously standing with the rest of the prostitutes in the corner where I avoided looking. Having her walk straight for me changed that. She was medium height and had on a really tight dress that barely started covering her thighs. She had on black boots. After the initial realization of what was happening, I was surprised by my reaction. I always thought I would be repulsed by the thought of being with a prostitute, but she was incredibly attractive. Her face even looked kind. I felt an instant dread that I would make her feel ugly and rejected if I didn't go along with what she was about to propose. As a guy raised to try and be a gentleman, my knee-jerk reaction was to always be deferential towards women, even if it inconvenienced me. I distinctly remember thinking to myself, "I guess I'm gonna have to do this. Do I have $50?" The combination of being very attracted to this gorgeous female and the dangerous aspect of the situation proved essentially irresistible. The woman was almost to my car and began to speak, but as I was about to walk and speak with her near the right headlight of my car, I saw Spanish letters in the air right in front of me, *Su puerta es la entrada al infierno* in cursive letters. That's a version of Proverbs 7:27, referring to a prostitute: "Her house is the way to hell, going down to the chambers of death." I know for a fact that I would have paid that woman and had sex with her, but after I physically saw that, I turned without speaking a word and got in the car to get gasoline somewhere else. I felt extremely rude and guilty that I had ignored the nice young lady kind enough to approach me. This was the biggest surprise for me, the horrible anxiety and discomfort I felt at having to reject her. As I drove off, I called my dad immediately and told him to keep me occupied on the phone. "If I don't keep talking with you, I'm going to end up sleeping with a prostitute." "Don't do it son!" was his reply, with gratitude and relief. My whole reaction took me completely by surprise, making me realize how difficult it is to say no to a woman. As men we are socialized to be deferential towards women. Biologically we are also programmed to take as many opportunities as we can. It goes against our every instinct to reject a woman who makes herself sexually available to us with no strings attached. As I kept driving after hanging up with dad on the cell phone, I remembered judging Magic Johnson when he got AIDS from a prostitute back in the day. My judgment turned to compassion. Whether those yellow, cursive letters were a true supernatural event or they were psychosomatic, it doesn't matter. Right at that moment God kept me safe and stopped me from acting. Everything inside me demanded that I have sex with that beautiful woman, but I was thankfully prevented from it. That's the only time something supernatural like that has ever happened to me, and I suspect it will be the last. God hasn't kept me from other mistakes and I often wonder, why that one in particular? Of course I'll never know this side of Eternity. The best course of action is to avoid the temptation instead of relying on the hand of God to intervene. It seems that He has decided to give us freedom to learn the hard way most of the time. Some don't believe in true Free Will. Even if one doesn't believe in it, we all have to live as if we have it. Trust me, you can easily fall into temptation. Just avoid it in the first place. We aren't as strong or as faithful as we think we are. With warm regards from your affectionate uncle, Tio Edwin.

In any moment of decision, the best thing you can do is the right thing. The worst thing you can do is nothing. —Theodore Roosevelt,

Twenty years from now you will be more disappointed by the things that you didn't do than by the ones you did do. So throw off the bowlines. Sail away from the safe harbor. Catch the trade winds in your sails. Explore. Dream. Discover. —H. Jackson Brown Jr.

Dear Nephew,

I left Nashville and St. Louis and began studies for my second masters degree in 2005. I was in my mid-twenties and making positive changes. I got involved in a church right away, and made some friends in school within months of my arrival. The first year, three women asked me out. This had never happened before, but during my mid-twenties, women started approaching me often. While we as men are attracted mainly to physical beauty, women are attracted to attitude, accomplishment, and potential. Experience can't be improvised, so the more accomplished and mature you are, the more attractive you become. However, this was new to me. I didn't know how to react. I told the first girl that I didn't know how I felt. She was quite physically attractive, but that's all I knew. We agreed to go on a date, but I had my apprehensions. She was younger, she struck me as a little naive and immature. I never gave her a definite answer until she approached me and said that somebody else had once rejected her. "He never told me he didn't like me, but told me as much in so many words." She said that sentence with such sadness that I felt horrible. Right at that moment I told her that, since I still didn't know, we should just be friends. I was also unsure of the second girl who expressed interest in me. Once during a get-together with mostly male friends of the church group, she said in the girliest voice imaginable that she didn't have a gag reflex. She sat on the floor, opened her mouth, and repeatedly slid a huge, oversized pencil in and out of her mouth as far into her throat as humanly possible. As you might imagine, the guys in the room were transfixed, myself included. There was another woman (our Bible study leader) in the group of about 8, and she quickly told her "alright, we get the point, that's enough. Give me the pencil." After losing the pencil to the Bible study leader, she giddily smiled and asked all of us "isn't that wild?" We nervously looked around, unsure of what to say. I couldn't tell whether she was aware of the sexual connotations or whether her girlish enthusiasm was genuine. I suppose I'll never know, but the strange episode was hot. She called me on one occasion to spend time together and say she had feelings for me, but I did the same thing I had done with the previous girl. I was not decisive. Eventually, it led to a blow-up between us where she told me I was making her feel bad. I finally just told her I was not going to be dating her. The third girl that approached me was a wonderful girl. Her walking was impaired and she had to use walkers. I had always gone out of my way to open doors for her and help her out. On Valentine's day she sent me a little heart-gram over Facebook. The social network was still new and this year there was an option to send little Valentine icons for a dollar. She purchased a little bear with the subject "Please bear with me," saying she wished to be more than friends. I'd never considered her romantically, but if she wanted to go out with me, why would I assume I wasn't going to like her? I told her I would be more than happy to take her out and spend time together. However, I made it clear that I had not considered her romantically and we would just have to wait and see. I picked her up and took her to dinner and a movie, paying for everything (as men should), even though she had asked me out. In light of what happened before, after that first date I decided to be candid with her and said I did not feel a romantic connection. "Who knows why chemistry happens between some people and not others?" She seemed quite hurt by this and separated herself from the group from then on. I felt bad, but really had nothing to be ashamed of. With these three experiences, it became clear to me how hard it is for women to feel rejection. Most never learn how to deal with the constant rejection that we as men have to get used to. Under normal circumstances, I would not have rejected any of them. However, I had been through so much drama when leaving St. Louis, that I was looking to date someone special who would understand me, not just a beautiful, fun girl for the moment. As you grow as a person, you'll start to notice the effect you have on the women around you. When I was younger I assumed women were the only ones who had power to affect our feelings. Most of us might not cause an instant reaction on women by our physical appearance, but once a woman gets to know how you are and what your capabilities are, there is a real chance a woman will become attracted to you. Don't be surprised by or afraid of that, but do be aware that you might have to communicate directly on occasion and reject a woman. It's always painful; there's something about it that always seems unnatural. Unfortunately, it's a necessity sometimes. With warm regards from your affectionate uncle, Tio Edwin.

When you find your path, you must not be afraid. You need to have sufficient courage to make mistakes. Disappointment, defeat, and despair are the tools God uses to show us the way. —
Paulo Coelho

Everything we hear is an opinion, not a fact. Everything we see is a perspective, not the truth. —Marcus Aurelius

Dear Nephew,

I was fortunate enough to study abroad; if you get the chance, jump on the opportunity. It's incredible how much you learn traveling. While I studied in London, I struck up a friendship with the janitors in the college. They were all foreigners—from Spain, Italy, and Romania, mostly—and they all lived in a large house inside the school complex. There were around 10 people in the house at any given time. Since I struck a friendship with a few of the janitors, they invited me to stay in their extra bedroom. It became a wonderful adventure. On weekends we traveled to different countries in Europe on the cheap. We also explored London as much as possible, sometimes dealing with normal roommate drama. On the last day there, right before leaving for the U.S., we were having breakfast and one of the girls in the house I had barely spoken to slipped me a note. I'll call her Mara. It was odd because I couldn't recall speaking with her. I had only hung out and traveled with the outgoing members of the group, not because I wanted to ignore anybody, but because there were only so many hours in the day to enjoy. I read the letter on the bus to the airport. She noticed that I was a fun person and that we should keep in touch. We emailed for years after I got home. At first the emails were infrequent and friendly, but after months of communication, we began to get close. We wrote regular, physical letters, and wrote on a notebook we sent back and forth. We would decorate it with pictures, drawings, and photos for each other. I enjoyed it very much. At one point she wrote we could be more than friends. Over two years had passed. I decided to ask my parents to help me buy a plane ticket one summer between classes in order to give it a shot. My parents warned me not to get married in a rush, and if I did propose, that she would be moving to the U.S., not me to Europe. I was still in my early 20s and she was about 9 years older. I returned to London and spent two weeks just hanging out, living in the same building I had stayed in years before. In her letters, Mara had described the working environment like a nightmare. All her work colleagues were immature and disagreeable. Her roommates weren't fair to her because she was shy. As soon as I got to London and re-connected with some of the same people who'd been there before (as well as some new ones) it became clear that her co-workers were perfectly friendly people. I had expected to walk into an insane asylum by the way Mara had described them. We went out every night of the first week, but conversation with Mara was different than our communication over letters. Besides being shy, she was blunt to the point of cruelty. She mentioned how my Caribbean Spanish accent sounded so low-class it was like a child speaking. I seemed immature when I got excited about doing something with her. It was bizarre. Every night I bought us expensive tickets to a different show, restaurant, and travel expenses, but not only did she never thank me, on several occasions she complained that the seats weren't to her liking, among other petty complaints. I thought I would make the best of it and ignore the negativity, but it didn't change. I'd had enough and told her that between me and my parents we spent over $7,000 for me to travel there and buy her all these experiences and gifts so we could spend time together. Couldn't she at least be a little grateful? Following my sincere pleading, she told me I was too immature, because a real man would not be so apologetic and grovel to her. She needed someone who would be secure enough to take what she was saying and give it back. Someone who wouldn't take her crap and fight back. I decided to spend the last week with the other people in the house and avoid her. We had a wonderful time. The situation was like a movie thriller. I thought all her co-workers were lunatics because I'd only read about them through her eyes. It was a sobering realization of what one of my cousins used to say: "the paper holds what you put on it." Long-distance dating cannot work for long periods of time. Before I left London, I gave Mara a note like she had given me so many years before. On this note, however, I told her what a disappointment this trip had been. Few people had treated me so disrespectfully in my life, and I never wanted to speak to her again. Years later we reconnected on a social network and patched things up a bit. While the messages were always cordial, I made it a point to never share much of myself with her again. I would never discover what made her behave in such a hurtful manner when I was willing to travel for love, although this was no big sacrifice because I no longer cared. With warm regards from your affectionate uncle, Tio Edwin.

The secret source of humor itself is not joy but sorrow. —Mark
Twain

*The most sophisticated people I know - inside they are all
children.* —Jim Henson

Dear Nephew,

I had just started my second Masters when I decided
to start teaching salsa dancing on a weekly basis for extra
income. I found a local business that gave me space, and
the whole endeavor went great. Students started coming
right away. One of the students was a girl I'll call
Claudette. She was blonde, cute, and very bubbly. I was
attracted to her right away. I thought I'd had bad luck with
women by being the nice guy (particularly after that
summer in London with Mara), so I decided to be the "bad
boy" with her. I would tease her mercilessly, give her
imperative commands in public, call her to say I was
picking her up in 15 minutes (without having given her any
prior warning), tease her about being fat, etc. I did all this
with a lot of humor and indifference. Most times she
seemed amused and laughed, either genuinely or nervously.
I always kept her off balance, never revealing what I felt.
After several months, we were spending a lot of time
together. I kept up my act even after several incidents that
took me by surprise. The first was during a random visit I
gave her. The details of the date are murky now (it's been
so many years) but what stands out in my mind was
walking her up to her room. At the door she pushed me

back, held me against the door, and started kissing me. I was flattered and happy, but I decided to keep up the act. I laughed a bit, told her to slow her horses, and made a rude comment about her not knowing whether I wanted to be kissed or not. Of course, I said all this with a smile in a teasing manner. I said bye and walked out to my car. I had to pick up a friend, and had timed it so that I couldn't spend that much time with her. This seemed like a jerk thing to do, so I scheduled it that way. I suppose that technically, she never did ask me whether I wanted to be kissed, so was that an assault? Today's standards really have no practical application in real life. The relationship took a hard turn when we were in her room watching an instructional dance video. She forcefully pushed me onto her bed and started kissing me. Her legs wrapped around me as best she could, she began undressing and touching me. I stopped the whole thing and told her that I couldn't do it. "Why doesn't anyone ever want to have sex with me?!" was her reply. It took me aback. Besides the obvious thought of "how many guys has this girl tried to get with?", I felt put down. I got up and tried to ease the tension. We finished the video and politely left, but I knew that things had to change. The next time together, I decided to come clean. I will never forget it. We were eating in a KFC. I told her I couldn't stop thinking about her and what she meant to me. I had been consciously trying to keep her interested by being so intense and forward—so bad— but I explained it was an act. I wanted to know how she felt about me. That was the moment I realized this "bad boy" act is not for me. With a smirk she told me, "Well Edwin, I think you're a good time." I felt disappointed and sad, but there was nothing I could do. In an instant, I decided to continue my act and my facial expression changed instantly. I went back to the character I had created, and, bringing my head slightly back, I said cynically "man, you're just cold and heartless, aren't you?" I went back to my "see-if-I-care" attitude and smoothly transitioned the conversation away from where I had taken it. In the car driving her back, I once again commented on how sexy she was, but also pointed out that she should cover up her kankles (she was self conscious about how thick her ankles were, even though she was quite beautiful). That was the last time I spent time with her. We were really at an impasse of my making. She had not really gotten to know me, she had only known an act I had put on for months in order to keep her interested. In a way it did feel nice to be considered the bad influence for once, as I had always been so responsible and straitlaced. However, I just couldn't do it anymore. I am glad I teased her a little bit and played that role at first, but I regret keeping it up for so long. I should've let her know how I felt before she tried to make the relationship physical. I was still in a place in my life where I was dating for fun and never considered how getting emotionally attached with someone could be a waste of time. Opportunity cost is something that never even entered my mind. The time I was spending with Claudette was time I could have been making other friends, or working on my business (everything I earned teaching salsa I was spending on her and then other girls). I should have been focusing on improving myself and my life. It was way too much time and money spent on one person that I barely knew. I have dozens of examples of this, unfortunately. I hope you won't have to go through it even once. With kind regards from your affectionate uncle, Tio Edwin.

Sincerity - if you can fake that, you've got it made. —George
Burns

*A man with outward courage dares to die. A man with inner
courage dares to live.* —Lao Tzu

Dear Nephew,

My trips back to the old country were times when I
met new people, both guys and girls, in order to not
completely lose touch with our culture. I was on an
extended trip visiting my family in my hometown one
summer in my early twenties when I met Iris from the
nearby town of Yauco. I was staying with my grandmother
and every day I would walk to school and around the
neighborhood just to look around. One night, I heard some
young people singing praise and worship music from a
house nearby. I went over and introduced myself. It was
some undergraduates who were living in a Christian house
for college girls. I sang with them a bit as the sun was
going down and explained I wasn't doing anything that
summer. They told me I should stop by for some food
whenever I wanted. I took them up on the offer and it
turned out wonderfully. I was doing my first masters degree
at the time, and so I wasn't very much older than them. I
would call in if I heard anybody hanging out (there were no
door bells) and many times I'd get invited in for some fried
food. Iris was really quite delightful and a great person to
be around. I started calling for her every night and we
would take walks around the neighborhood. At one point

my parents came to visit and we all went to the beach together. During one of the last nights I was going to be there, we took a walk at night to some fountains in a plaza. It was a beautiful night and she said she was a little tired and cold. I wrapped my arm around her, and after she lay her head on my shoulder, I looked at her and we kissed. One would think this would make for a wonderful night, but unfortunately it didn't. I had to open my big mouth. Instead of enjoying the moment, I felt like I needed to go out of my way to treat her right. She was a church girl and I wanted to be straight forward. I told her about my past girlfriend Flor (from Mexico) and that I had not been "faithful" to her after we dated long distance for some years. I told her that I was afraid of doing the same thing to her and that I would rather be upfront about it. I honestly wanted to do the right thing, especially because she had been so sweet and loving towards me. As soon as I mentioned that, she began to cry. "Why would you lead me on if you knew you weren't going to be interested in me?" she said. I was dumbfounded by her crying. I hadn't planned on kissing her. To this day I don't know exactly why I told her so much about my past. I was interested in her. She assumed I told her that in order not to be with her, but I brought it up as a way to be serious about the situation. As soon as she began to cry, I froze. I was tongue tied and by not taking charge of the situation, I let her assume the worst. While I was hoping to talk about expectations and how we could plan on traveling often to see each other, I saw her steeling herself against me with an immediate change in demeanor. This change really intimidated me. I wish I would have anticipated that death stare in order to be emotionally ready. Her face got serious. She separated herself physically from me, assumed a rigid posture, and said, "Well, I suppose we better walk back," she said. It was night time and not safe for her to walk alone, so I walked her back, silence and awkwardness overtaking what had been a beautiful night. I tried to undo the damage that had been done by my comments, but it was to no avail. She treated me like a playboy for the entire half hour it took to walk her home; the very thing I was trying to avoid by being honest. We went our separate ways and never kept in touch. Years later we randomly ran into each other at a wedding. She spoke to me with the same discomfort she had with me years before when my honesty made her cry beside the fountain. She was married to a pastor and, in her mind, she had dodged a major bullet with me. Lesson learned: be slow to talk and quick to listen. Like my mother used to tell me, "What does she care about your past? Your father doesn't know anything about whoever I dated before him, and there's no need for him to know." Wise words. Not everything needs to be said when first getting to know someone, or ever, for that matter. There's no need to be talking about your past when it isn't necessary. Let your actions speak about you and who you are now. If you are going to explain negative things about yourself, make sure you explain your purpose. "I want to tell you this so you know I'm serious about wanting to date you. I want us to make this work." That would've been the way to start that conversation by the fountain. With warm regards from your affectionate uncle, Tio Edwin.

To catch a husband is an art; to hold him is a job. —Simone de Beauvoir

Do not fear failure rather fear not trying. —Roy T. Bennett

Dear Nephew,

I was surprised by how things developed with Lynn. I met her while studying for my second Master's degree. She was a sexy Chicana studying for her graduate terminal degree. I loved her accent and the way she always dressed to impress, like many Latinas do. I was obviously interested in her and didn't hide it, but she didn't see me the same way. I didn't let that deter me, though, and whenever I had a moment I would stop by her place to say hi. I started hanging out with her group of friends to be around her, and she seemed to like that. This led to an awkward situation with one of her female friends that assumed I was interested in her. I should not have spent so much time with her friends to ingratiate myself with her. Too many unspoken complications made things unnecessarily difficult. I was focused on Lynn. Since I was intimidated by her, I treated it as a challenge to knock on her door—I was doing it for me. I knew that she wasn't going to magically fall in love with me, but I liked her and I liked her company. If she was willing to give it to me, why not? I never pressured her to date me, we simply spent time together. At first I would knock on her door and say that I was driving by so I thought I would say hello. If there was an event at her church or at the University that she was going to, I attended and greeted her warmly. I never hovered or demanded her time. Unknowingly, my focus on conquering my fear of talking to her turned my actions into confident pursuit, rather than desperate chasing. There is a subtle difference between the two that women can feel immediately. I didn't approach her from a sense of inferiority. She slowly warmed up to me. It got to the point where I would go over and watch a movie at her apartment at least once a week. One thing led to another after some time like this. After a particularly interesting conversation, I kissed her on her couch. She kissed me back and, after embracing, she asked me if I wanted her to disrobe completely as she took off her blouse, revealing beautiful, lacy, black underwear. I couldn't believe this was happening. We hadn't even defined the relationship, it had simply happened naturally from spending so much time together. After quickly stopping her from disrobing further, I told her that I didn't want to see her naked and to keep her blouse on. That night the relationship had jumped from zero to 100 in three seconds and I didn't want things to get out of hand. We weren't a couple, so I wanted to take it slower. As she put her clothes back on, she said, "You know, I didn't like you like this in the beginning. Your persistence is what really won me over." That was incredible to me because, other than the enjoyment of making out a little bit, she had not won me over yet. I was physically attracted to her, but that was all. We as men are attracted to most women, so physical attraction isn't that special. Things had gotten way too intense before I even knew her. Since she was never interested in me, she never shared much about herself. This entire time we had talked about current events, what was happening with her friends, the movies we had watched, some school events, etc. I appreciated the witty conversation, but I didn't even know where her family was from, if she had any siblings, what she wanted to do with her degree—nothing. After that night I never felt such a strong need to spend time with her again like I had before. My visits grew more infrequent. We were both busy, after all. We would say hi every once in a while, and it was always lovely to speak with her. While we were casual and friendly, I stopped pushing for a deeper relationship. We kept in touch on social media, but she moved and we never interacted after that. The whole thing had been a wonderful experience that didn't last due to a lack of intention on my part. Since my only goal was to face the fear of speaking with her and getting her to spend time with me, once that goal was met, I left the whole situation in limbo. The girl was hanging out with me. Now what? We were both finishing up school. We believed our lives were not in a place to prioritize anything else other than school. That attitude is something I regret. Your personal life is still important, even if you're going to the best school or working the best job in the world. We didn't think that way, however, and the moment passed. I also didn't realize getting physical would make my desire to get to know her wane. I made a point today to see if we were still connected through social media. We are. It had been at least 5 years since the last time I checked. Perhaps our families can meet in the future. It would be nice to catch up and see where life has taken her. Our children could play together while she and my wife chat. With kind regards from your affectionate uncle, Tio Edwin

You and I are too wise to woo peaceably. —*Shakespeare, Much ado about nothing*

The meeting of two personalities is like the contact of two chemical substances: if there is any reaction, both are transformed. —*Carl Gustav Jung*

Dear Nephew,

My mother suggested I pay attention to the Bible study leader from the last letter. I'll call her Billie. She was single and very attractive. How hadn't I noticed her before? A beautiful face, smile, and hour-glass figure that ended in an AppleBottom jeans commercial. I asked her out, but she resisted, asking "Do you know how old I am?" I replied that I did not care. "I'm 32 years old." Almost 10 years older than me, but I was glad. Here was a woman who would probably not play games. Her life story was fascinating. Fluent in Arabic after spending time in the Middle East, this typical midwestern woman joked she wanted to be a third wife; that's the fun wife in polygamous marriages. It was fascinating to talk with her, but she refused to date me. For months I attempted to show her that I was worth dating. Friends helped me serenade her with "Life could be a dream" in tight, 3-part harmony. It took us weeks of practice. When we finally serenaded her, she refused to come down, sending her mother instead. I gave her mother the flowers and candy – nothing else to do but walk away defeated in front of my friends. About a week later, just as I gave up hope, Billie wrote to me expressing she might consider a relationship. I jumped on the chance, and it was a typical beginning. She was so anxious when I first kissed her that she grabbed my shoulders and forcefully pushed me away. Quickly realizing what she had done, she pulled me back by my shirt and started kissing me. Two seconds into the kiss, she stuck her tongue in my mouth so far I had to stop everything and ask "What the heck was that?!" I was concerned yet outwardly laughing at the same time. She apologized and explained that she hadn't been with someone for years and was so anxious she panicked. I kissed her gently and reassured her that she didn't need to be nervous. It turned out to be a sweet moment. Things were going great, but four months in, the mood changed. The first major fight we had was in her house in front of her parents, to my horror. She was showing me old pictures when one with her sister came up. I complimented Billie for how she looked in it—she was wearing shorts that accentuated her figure. She asked if I thought her sister was prettier. Of course, I was a little uncomfortable with the question, but she was much sexier than her sister and I was not lying when I said that. Billie's figure was amazing. Mentioning that escalated the situation further, however. Billie felt like her butt looked "obscene," she explained. It was too big and stuck out too much. Her sister had always been the attractive one. I could not believe what I was hearing. I told her men typically like fuller figures like hers and she had a much better figure than her sister. She was having none of it. It got to the point where she was screaming at me at the top of her lungs right there in the living room. Her parents were in the next room, passively listening, and I asked her to please step outside the house to continue this "conversation." The whole thing was unbelievable. How could things escalate so quickly over me complimenting her figure? I later learned that she had been clinically depressed. About 3 months into dating me, she stopped taking her medication, assuming I would not like it. Now things made sense. Near the four-month mark in our relationship, we began going through intense swings—from ecstasy, to depression, to outright hostility. It was exhausting. I never knew if what I said would send her into a mood. On one occasion, she got rejected for a job. She read me the rejection letter and, as we sat in her room, began crying. I hugged her, but the crying deepened until she began sobbing uncontrollably. I held her for ten minutes before I started looking at the clock. Fifteen minutes went by, half an hour, 45 minutes… I held her for an hour and a half of uncontrollable sobbing by the time she calmed down. Finally, I gently looked at her and said, "Billie, you need to be stronger than this. It was just a job! You can always apply to another one. There are plenty of jobs." After months and months of having these jarring mood swings, she finally went back on the anti-depressants, but the damage was done. Once again, I was about to leave town because my masters studies were complete. We agreed to continue the relationship long-distance, but after a bad fight during a visit—complete with shouting so loud that it distorted her voice— I'd had enough and broke it off in yet another intense episode. After traveling, I settled into my new apartment and began studying for my doctoral degree. Weeks went by. I missed her. The constant up and down can become addictive and easily confused with love. It would take time to realize I saw that roller coaster—the fear, intense conflict, depressing episodes, and elation when we reconciled—as the way I felt love now. Sudden conflict makes you feel the moment intensely. You can't live your life in a perpetual roller coaster. You have a road to walk. Get with someone who will walk with you, and not keep you going through emotional upheavals. Like a drug, it can be exciting, but devastating. With warm regards from your affectionate uncle, Tio Edwin.

Not what we have but what we enjoy constitutes our abundance.
—Epicurus

A proud man is always looking down on things and people; and,
of course, as long as you are looking down, you cannot see
something that is above you. —C.S. Lewis

Dear Nephew,

A new city called for new experiences, so I decided
to try online dating where I met Yvette. Within two emails,
she suggested we meet at the mall. This was refreshing to
say the least. I had tried online dating before, but most
times this meant endless emailing back and forth while
planning to meet in the unknown future. After 6 months of
emailing, when the time to meet in person finally came, the
girl was nothing like her pictures suggested and I would
end up not enjoying my time with her at all. Six months
wasted. I was glad Yvette wanted to meet immediately. We
hit it off right away after meeting at the mall and had a
relationship that lasted for four months. She was taller than
me (which I liked) and beautiful. We went dancing in a
club the first night, something that really turned her on. She
put her elbows around my neck, her eyes got serious with
her mouth slightly open, and she stared into my eyes
intensely. We went to my apartment afterwards, still feeling
the excitement of the moment, and with a smile she began
kissing me. I thought it best to cut the date off after a few
moments of this because things were getting hot and heavy
really quickly, and we had just met! After talking, I drove
her back in disbelief. Here was a beautiful, exciting chick

—beautiful tattoos on her back and left thigh—quite taller than me, and a gorgeous body. She had experimented with drugs in high school, but was off them and became quite religious, trying her best to live life as a christian. I called her the next day and she mentioned how much she appreciated me not taking advantage of how turned on she was. A man that can dance has a natural advantage, she mentioned. She was over the moon, and it showed. Everything was going well, but more than a month into the relationship, I noticed I didn't know where she worked. She hid from me that she was a janitor and came from a very poor family. We are talking about real poverty. She grew up without a shower in her house, only taking baths; the first shower she ever took was during her late teens, and she remembered how awesome the experience was. She was afraid that I would think less of her, but her fears were misplaced. I admired her very much for her work ethic and how far she'd come. I'd never met someone from a rural area of the U.S. who had grown up in such poverty. While her family was poor materially, they were rich in love. Hanging out with them was wonderful. We played games, were silly, talked about anything and everything, went to the lake… it was really a lovely family. My favorite game was "the ax game," where we would throw axes at a huge, wooden bullseye on a tree. Going to the lake with her family was great too. She and her sisters were all gorgeous. It was like hanging out with really fun models in bikinis who were kind, loving towards everyone around them, and uninhibited conversationalists. The first time driving back from the lake, Yvette changed into her underwear under her shirt while sitting on the passenger seat in my car as quickly as she could. I'll never forget her giggling while she looked at me with a look that said, "what?" and "did you like that?" at the same time. Unfortunately, I could not get emotionally close to her for a few reasons. I was still missing Billie. I missed how well-educated, well-traveled, and well-read she was. I also felt guilty because four months into the relationship I started feeling superior to Yvette, even though I didn't want to. I had finished two Masters degrees and was completing my doctorate. She had a high school diploma. I missed discussing issues that required study and travel to understand. Eventually, I avoided certain subjects I liked in order to preserve the harmony we had, which I loved. I knew that I wanted more than just a beautiful, fun girl. I also wanted to discuss international travel, food, political topics, denominational and religious differences, or other subjects of no interest to her. The tipping point came when we were reading a book together. It was her turn to read and she came to a number. It was 16,428 if I recall correctly. She came to the number and stopped. Instead of pronouncing it, she said, "one, six, four, two, eight." I reflexively uttered a sound, surprised and not knowing what to say. What kind of a high school system graduates students unfamiliar with numbers? American education needs to improve. She was a really smart woman, so it was clearly not completely her failing. I told her to repeat after me, which she did, and we read the number. Not much math is needed to balance a checkbook, she explained, and we moved on with the reading. Even though I didn't make a big deal of the moment to her, at that moment I decided to break up with her. I met her at her second-story apartment and sat down in her kitchen. It was a rather quick conversation where I told her I really liked her, but needed to see other people. I still wasn't over somebody (thinking of Billie) and it wasn't fair to her. She got very upset. After a bewildered look she gasped "why?!" and cried. In anger she blurted out "but I love you!!" I will never forget her expression of anger and sadness. I thought I was doing the right thing, but I was disappointed in myself. I was going to miss her excitement and flirty energy. Years later I learned that Yvette pursued an art major in college. Looking back, I did the wrong thing. Witty sophistication can be learned, but there are more important things that can't be—kindness, flirtatiousness, a love of life. I ignored all that because she couldn't read a number and I missed a woman that made me miserable. What was wrong with me? Your affectionate uncle, Tio Edwin.

You are controlled by the one who makes you angry. —Lao Tzu

Fortune favors the bold. —Latin proverb

Dear Nephew,

After Yvette, I connected with Billie again. She decided to visit over a weekend and things went well at first. We ate out, watched movies, took walks and talked a lot. The last night she was there the situation took a horrible turn, however. She confessed she had been sexual with someone else right before coming to see me and I became livid. Why was she with me then? I had never been so angry. As I got up to stand, I grabbed a chair, wanting to break it on her. I had endured her insults, her shouting; her crying sometimes for hours over nothing; constantly walking on eggshells. I felt betrayed, angry, and concerned. Had she exposed me to an STD? I left the chair on the floor and kicked it hard. While pacing back and forth, I asked her how she could've done that. She began to cry, apologizing. The man was a talker and had seduced her. I shouted "get out of my apartment!" For the first time in our relationship, I was the one shouting. I threw her stuff out into the hall. It was the middle of the night, but I didn't care. I locked the door behind me as she stood crying in the apartment hallway. She began lightly tapping on the door. "Edwin please… where am I going to go? I have nowhere to stay." Eventually I agreed to let her sleep in my apartment until the next morning when I drove her to the airport. At the airport I told her I never wanted to see her again. That would be dramatic enough if it were the end of the story, but of course there is more. A few days later, Billie began emailing and calling. At first I ignored it, but eventually I answered. She had decided to move to my city. I insisted—in fact sometimes shouted— that I never wanted to see her again. She didn't care. Even if I never spoke to her, she would move to be around me. She had no family or friends there. She could do whatever she wanted, but I would never see her again, I said. I had cooled off by the time she moved and regularly answered her emails. She wanted me to meet her at a restaurant, to which I reluctantly agreed. After all, she didn't know anybody in the entire city. At that meeting, I agreed to help her move into her apartment. I couldn't let a woman carry all her furniture alone, after all. This went on for several weeks until—you guessed it— she convinced me to give the relationship one more shot. It was a disaster. We ended up having a relationship through the winter of 2008 until 2009 that was pathological. I won't go into details, but the cycle of ups and downs came back with a vengeance. It seemed we stayed together to see how much we could hurt each other. One time she said if I left her she should just kill herself. After that incident, whenever we fought, I would hide all the knives. She would make me feel guilty for not spending time with her. After using that tactic on me one afternoon, I met her in a restaurant. After some awkward conversation, she noticed a blond hair on my shoulder. That was the end. Billie accused me of cheating and of being a womanizer. The hair was from a singer at school I accompanied on the piano as an assignment. I'll call her Carmela. Truth be told, I had become attracted to Carmela, but I had not planned to do anything about it, given how messed up my life was. I resented Billie speaking so harshly to me, especially over a hair on my shirt. That would be the last time I saw her. She continued calling me and belittling me on phone calls. Her emails became increasingly nasty and combative. I told her to stop calling and writing. Finally, one day she refused to leave me alone, so I called the cops. I asked them to tell her I did not wish to have any more contact. In her last message, she accused me of being a horrible, uncaring man, who didn't care she was up here all alone and didn't appreciate the sacrifices she made in moving. A deep sadness came over me for a short while right after this incident. Two years of my life trying to make a relationship work, and the only things left were resentment and a nagging fear she would try to hurt me or herself. I should have ended that relationship with the first red flag. Her reactions to anything that upset her were so verbally violent towards me that they would send me into an internal panic and numbness that lasted for days. Many women don't understand how impactful verbal confrontation is for us men. We get into a state where we can't think straight and need some time to process. This is something she seldom gave me. She thought that we needed to keep talking non-stop until we both felt better. When all else failed, she believed that being sexual with me would fix the problem. I didn't know how to deal with such dysfunction, and I carried around scars for years because of it. If you're walking on eggshells for more than a day while you're dating, break up. It's not worth it. Like they say in business:

hire slowly and fire quickly. Give yourself one red flag incident before you start to consider breaking up with someone. It'll save you time and heartache. With Warm regards from your affectionate uncle, Tio Edwin.

Rarely do great beauty and great virtue dwell together. —
Petrarch

*Appreciation is a wonderful thing. It makes what is excellent in
others belong to us as well.* —*Voltaire*

Dear Nephew,

My interactions with Joanie were always wonderful
and should've been an indication of what I longed to have
in my life. I wouldn't realize this for years, unfortunately. I
met Joanie as a freshman my junior year of undergraduate
school. We went to the same department and had pleasant
conversations every now and then, but nothing more. Three
years after I graduated we found each other on a social
network and kept in touch. I'd always thought she was very
wise and it was nice to get back in touch. We spoke on the
phone occasionally and wrote each other messages. She
was studying for her masters degree on the West Coast
while I did my second masters degree in South Dakota. Her
conversation was the stuff I had always dreamed of:
beautiful, sophisticated, well-read, challenging, yet kind
and looking for the best in others. Joanie was one of the
most cultured people I'd ever met, but she had never been
forward about her feelings towards me or even hinted that
she might have any. By this time in my life this was
completely unusual as I was getting used to girls being
open about their feelings and sometimes even demanding
that I spend time with them. One girl even accused me of
discriminating against her because I wasn't going to sleep

with her. I can't emphasize enough the depth of admiration I had for Joanie. Whenever I worked up the courage to call her, we would talk for long stretches of time about current events, her opinions about certain books, and discuss how certain theological beliefs applied to our every-day lives. When Billy finally approached me after her initial rejection, I gave the relationship with her a shot and stopped communicating so much with Joanie, but found that I would consistently want to reach out to her. One night I spoke with Joanie on the phone for about an hour outside of Billy's house after Billy blew up at me. I didn't know Billy had stopped taking medication for depression and would end up screaming at me at the top of her lungs. After some small talk, Joanie realized the situation, calmed me down, and talked me through how I should deal with it. She always pushed me to trust in God. She probably doesn't remember those phone calls, but they were important in my life. I continued communicating with her in that manner through two girlfriends. It's unbelievable when I think back on it. Because of this I suspect she firmly friend zoned me, although there were instances when she was definitely open to persuasion. She played her cards very close to her vest, which was incredibly attractive. The main problem I had was lack of resolve. I hinted at the possibility of us dating by saying that I would like to get to know her better, but that was all I said. Huge mistake. I approached Joanie too tentatively. With a high-quality woman who has things going on in her life, it is important to get her attention. Although I didn't realize it, I was doing a "back burner" situation. You never put it to yourself so bluntly, but you basically think: "I'll have contact with her every other week or so just to see if she's dating someone. If not, I'll see if she gets interested in me while keeping my personal options open." Don't ever let yourself get into a situation like this with a woman who you know is high quality. A beautiful girl who you admire, is kind to you, and you can't wait to have conversations with is rare. If you have any physical attraction for her, do not waste that opportunity. It will be a fear to overcome, but write yourself a script of what you want to say and find a way to tell her in person. Even if she doesn't reciprocate, you will be glad you did it. Oblique communication is fine at first, but not for years or even months. A woman who really expects a man to lead will flirt with you, be kind, and even be open to spending time alone, but don't expect her to cross the bridge of initiating a relationship defining talk (an RDT) as we used to call them back in the day. I was 25 years old, and girls were approaching me for a change. I was getting used to this dynamic, but wish I would've thought more about what I wanted, rather than letting myself go with the flow of whatever girl happened to become interested in me. Quality women like Joanie will be juggling her own admirers, so you have to cut through their noise by letting her know you want a relationship with her once you decide that. She will also not initiate an RDT with you, so you have to man up and discover how you feel, put it into words, and tell her face to face. No matter what happens from that point on, you will not regret it. Years later I traveled to visit Joanie on the West Coast for an extended weekend. She made sure to always have a girlfriend of hers with us, never led me on, and was an incredible pleasure to be around, as always. It was too late. The moment to seek a relationship with her had passed years before. I still held an incredible admiration for her, and thought that perhaps I should tell her? I'd gotten my first cell phone a few years before and had no sense of phone etiquette. I texted her, "Would you like to be my girlfriend?" Her reply was one word long. Please, don't ever be that lame. Tell her how you feel face to face. With Warm regards from your affectionate uncle, Tio Edwin.

The most painful thing is losing yourself in the process of loving someone too much, and forgetting that you are special too. — Ernest Hemingway

Don't think there are no crocodiles just because the water is calm. —African proverb

Dear Nephew,

A woman I'll call Paula was a dancer that oozed sophistication. She was a little taller than me, which I liked, and we grew close quickly. The first interaction with her mother should have been a red flag. She told me, rather coldly, "You better not get too attached to Paula. She can dismiss people fairly quickly from her life once she gets tired of them." Paula was a dominant personality. In a whirlwind, I ended up wasting a year of doctoral studies traveling with her instead of doing my work. Paula had a plan for our life. It was hard not to go along because she was so enthusiastic and charming—a real leader. After we won a local dance competition, dancing caused friction. She asked me not to dance with women—it made her feel insecure. When out dancing, I would sit and watch her dance with other men, and only dance with her. After six months of this, I asked when she was going to trust me. She admitted it was unfair, and decided to stop dancing with other men. When her friends found out she stopped dancing "because of me," everybody became concerned. They would whisper around us and emailed her asking about the situation. I sat out for six months—everybody saw I was not allowed to dance with women—yet nobody seemed concerned. In that double-standard I felt yet again how men of color are seen as a threat, particularly to white women. That Spring, there was another red-flag incident I chose to ignore. I decided to give her a surprise visit in a coffee shop where she was waitressing. She was busy, so I took a seat and waited. A young lady we both knew from dance walked in. I felt concern seeing this female, fearing what Paula would feel—another red-flag I couldn't recognize at the time. This young lady sat and talked with me for about 10 minutes. Paula became more irritated by the minute as she served customers. I ended the conversation as quickly as possible, trying to engage with Paula. She refused to talk. I stood up and approached her as she was taking some plates back to the kitchen. After asking why she was so angry, she shouted at the top of her lungs "because my boyfriend is a jerk!" Everyone in the small space was immobilized. She turned and walked away. She was the innocent victim and I was to blame. I lowered my head, walked out of the coffee shop, around the block and into my vehicle, feeling crushed. After calling that night and apologizing for making her feel insecure, she apologized for shouting. If the roles had been reversed, I would've been seen as a monster, but nobody thought twice about the situation, not even me. We began fighting almost weekly about not being engaged, at one point Paula telling me through tears, "every day that you don't propose to me is like a knife in my heart!" Her friends and family expected her to get married soon, and the pressure was constantly on me. Ironically, it was this constant pressure which didn't allow me to think clearly or know what I was feeling. The beginning of the end came when she proposed to me. We were in my condo. I needed to head to bed, so we said goodbye and I got in the shower, asking her to shut the door behind her. She opened the bathroom door and began chatting with me. Suddenly, she disrobed and jumped in the shower. The moment was shocking and intense. Half of me was embarrassed since I never thought my body was magazine worthy, but the other half was immobilized and reactive. After a moment of acting purely on animal instinct, she looked at me intensely and said, "Edwin, marry me." I froze once again with conflicting emotions, feeling manipulated. Our fights had been over this issue. I wanted to say yes, but not out of guilt, as I felt that I should have told her to get out of the shower. Instead of reacting, I didn't respond. After some small talk, we agreed to meet up the next day. The moment had passed. Looking to re-kindle the connection, the next day I told her my only condition for marriage was couples therapy. We would do it together to learn how to better communicate and avoid fights. My plan was to surprise her and buy a ring together after our first session. The morning of our scheduled therapy I was nervous but excited as I went to pick her up. As I waited outside in the jeep, I wondered what was taking so long. She finally texted me, "I don't want some therapist to tell me I'm crazy!" That was it. She had broken up with me in one text. It was scary how cruel she and her friends were to me so soon after she had asked me to marry her. She had obviously loved the idea of marriage for its own sake, rather than marrying me. How could I have ignored the red flags? I should have been able to figure out that Paula needed control of the relationship, including my actions and attitudes—an impossibility. I was often punished for sins of omission: I hadn't proposed yet; I did not act in public exactly like she wanted; I did not handle a situation forcefully enough; I wasn't as concerned as her on an issue. Each "sin of omission" could have been handled a million ways, but I had to find the needle in the haystack of possibilities and thread it perfectly for her not to be hurt or upset. A lot of American women belittle their men publicly. It's so common it passes as normal. I could never commit if I feared that from a woman, no matter how wonderful she might be, and Paula was truly wonderful. Better to be alone or continue serial dating, no matter how much I feared being lonely. I'll let the Bible describe the lesson: "It is better to live in a dessert land than with a quarrelsome and fretful woman" Proverbs 21:19. Your affectionate uncle, Tio Edwin.

So in everything, do to others what you would have them do to you, for this sums up the Law an the Prophets. —*Jesus of Nazareth, Matthew 7:12*

He who refuses to obey cannot command. —*African proverb*

Dear nephew,

A concept that is much more important to men than it is to women is respect. Of course, everybody wants and deserves to be respected. There are two types of respect we receive: immediate and earned. Since we don't live in an ideal world, disrespect and lack of courtesy will come at you from every direction. While you will be presented with many courses, books, seminars, and opportunities to learn how to make a great first impression—the type that gives you immediate respect—I believe this is not the right thing to focus on when looking to improve the way you interact with others. You'll read about psychological and sociological studies showing that a first impression is made within the first seconds of meeting. Someone will size you up and decide whether they like and respect you or not within moments of seeing you, even before anyone utters a word. The factors that determine if someone has immediate respect and attraction for you are too numerous to worry about this type of immediate respect. Your facial appearance, your height, your clothing, your stride, how fast or slow your movements are, how you interact with the space, people, and objects around you, how you react to the sights and sounds around you, how distracted you are, the temperature of your hands upon shaking, the length of the pauses between your statements…. the list is simply too long to worry too much about a first impression. Unfortunately, after a first impression people will tend to hold on to what they think about you due to confirmation bias. Nobody likes to be wrong, so we unconsciously start looking for things that confirm our first impressions of people. Others will unthinkingly do this to you and you will do the same to them. It's human nature. The people who are notorious for assuming the worst in others will have bad first impressions and will look for confirmation. Fortunately for us, those are exactly the people that we don't want to surround ourselves with. If you do happen to like a woman who for some reason has received a bad impression from you, you can always rely on earned respect. Earned respect requires a consistent demonstration of good faith and behavior on your part. Basically, you are demonstrating through time that you aren't the type of bad person she assumed you to be. You first made that bad impression because someone spilled a drink on you and you were looking to dry your hands. You had no intention of avoiding a hand shake with prolonged eye contact. The only way to consistently earn the respect of others around you is to always improve your character, habits, and routines. This is why focusing on earning the respect of those around you (especially those that you admire) is the best type of respect to focus on. Unfortunately, many women around you will be used to disrespecting the men in their lives, particularly in a romantic relationship. You might hear the phrase "respect is earned" from some women after they make an especially disrespectful comment, demand, or even scene against a man in their lives. Run away from these women like the plague. While there are 2 types of respect that one receives, there should be only one type given: unconditional. The only way we should treat everyone around us is with respect, whether they have earned it or not. Even if someone is being disrespectful towards us, the only way for the situation to improve for the better is by reacting respectfully towards them. Reacting disrespectfully to disrespect only deteriorates the situation faster. It also does nothing to build character in ourselves and make us stronger people. Of course, in a dating relationship, expectations and standards must be clearly communicated in order for the other person to know what you appreciate and consider respectful. If for some reason you don't like a woman walking on your left side when you are wearing purple, you must clearly communicate that as she might have no clue. If after one or two instances of blatant disrespect it is evident that a woman will never respect you, it is time to start forming a swift exit plan to stop seeing her. I've had quite a number of experiences where women protested and felt sad because I no longer wanted to see them. It's always a sad thing to have to do, but if it's necessary, don't be afraid of respectfully telling someone you never want to see them again. After all, someone that also deserves respect from you is yourself. Respectfully, from your affectionate uncle, Tio Edwin

Perhaps out there, somewhere, someone is sighing for your absence; and with this thought, my soul begins to breathe. —Petrarch

In forfeiting the sanctity of sex by casual, nondiscriminatory 'making out' and 'sleeping around,' we forfeit something we cannot well do without. There is dullness, monotony, sheer boredom in all of life when virginity and purity are no longer protected and prized. By trying to grab fulfillment everywhere, we find it nowhere. —Elisabeth Elliot

Dear Nephew,

Emotionally, I was exhausted from dating and went crazy. My motto was *Quiero quien me quiera* (I'll love whoever loves me). When I stopped caring, women approached me even more: most were single, some with boyfriends, some older, a few married. It was crazy. The first woman was older than my mother, but extremely hot. We knew it was temporary due to the age difference and only dated for a few months. She gave me strategies on how to attract younger women and encouraged me to approach them. The relationship was exciting and absolutely unorthodox. As a child I believed that women were angels, but that notion completely evaporated when a few married women were the most aggressive in pursuing me romantically. After some time of just going with the flow, I told the married women that I was not going to communicate with them anymore. I still craved companionship, but my conscience was working overtime. I wanted to be serious with my life, not be in pretend marriages anymore. I was done with serial dating one girl at a time and allowed myself to ask someone out whenever I felt an attraction. This went on for some months. One of the girls I dated got tired of not having me exclusively and kept asking why we couldn't date "normally" for a month. She couldn't be friends with me, otherwise. I had given so much in previous relationships that I could not give anymore. "So you're saying I'm so cool it's impossible for us to be friends if we aren't dating like you want? We don't have to be friends," I told her coldly. Threats bothered me, especially after I made my intentions clear from the beginning. I wish I had fostered such an internal locus of control younger, instead of going through so much heartbreak for it. Instead of quickly falling in line by putting the woman's wishes first, I moved on without a second thought. Unlike what I feared, I felt no regret about moving on. I was tired of dealing with demands. I even attended a few polyamorous lifestyle meetings. One curious experience was when an attractive, flirtatious woman was disappointed upon learning that I was not married. "Oh, I'm only interested in married men. I'm interested in being wife #2 and coming into an already established relationship. You seem like an awesome man, so please stay in touch and let me know when you're married." They disdainfully called the normal way of dating "the relationship escalator": flirt, date exclusively, get married, have children, work the same job till you die. That's the progression they rejected. While I never joined a polyamorous group, I was intrigued by it and continued dating multiple people at a time. There is no need to date only one person for years without knowing whether you want to marry them. I wish I had grown tired of these pretend marriages much sooner. While you're young, date if you'd like—"hang out," or whatever the kids call it now. However, consider applying this rule: if you go out with a woman alone, before you see her again you must see another woman. Tell her this before your first date. "I don't date exclusively" is all you need to say to start the conversation. Dating exclusively is a big step that shouldn't be taken lightly. Instead of falling into a quasi-marriage with someone you barely know, this will allow you to get to know people while avoiding the drama and deep emotional attachments that make it difficult to move on if you're not right for each other. It's a win/win. If you go out with Maria, remind her after the date that if she wants to go out again, it's your rule that you have to see somebody else, otherwise going out with her alone won't happen. Explain that it's for everybody's good, and that if she really wants to see you again, she might introduce you to her friend Emily. You will have to overcome your fear and have potentially awkward conversations, but you will notice the benefits right away. Everything is upfront. You are being honest with them and with yourself. The women with insecurities will drop out immediately. More adventurous, strong women will stay. Most importantly, you won't be emotionally invested in a quasi-marriage, avoiding situations where you end up having to pay for counseling and therapy to deal with issues. Dating should be fun and not complicated. If you need counseling while you're dating, it's time to break up. I would love to know the history of modern dating to understand how it became the complicated nonsense it has become. Have principles and rules for yourself, and stick with them. Don't just go with the flow like I did for so many years. Don't fall into a pretend marriage without first knowing the woman well and moving at your own, deliberate pace. If someone won't date you because she needs you all to herself before you've even learned her middle name, you've avoided a problem. With warm regards from your affectionate uncle, Tio Edwin.

A silly idea is current that good people do not know what temptation means. This is an obvious lie. Only those who try to resist temptation know how strong it is... A man who gives in to temptation after five minutes simply does not know what it would have been like an hour later. That is why bad people, in one sense, know very little about badness. They have lived a sheltered life by always giving in. —C.S. Lewis

When women go wrong, men go right after them. —Mae West

Dear Nephew

There is never going to be a perfect time for anything in life, much less the perfect time to express your love for someone. Even the week that I proposed to my wife, I was confronted by serious temptation from other women, including one episode I'll never forget. While my wife's kind, self-assured, and consistent kindness reeled me in, some women during this time made themselves available to me with no strings attached. I had been dating Rebecca exclusively for some time, and it was wonderful. Even if you want to be with someone exclusively, other women will always be a temptation, no matter how much you love someone. Candy (I'll call her) had asked me to give her a private dance lesson in her home. There was nothing unusual about this; I'd given hundreds of private dance lessons in homes by this point. After a little bit of dancing, she began to breathe heavily in an obviously sexual manner during my explanation of bachata. The music itself is quite beautiful and often danced closely, so it's not unusual for people to have feelings of intimacy, but this was another level. I continued the lesson politely, ignoring her provocative breathing and hoping the situation would just normalize. It did not. After pressing her breasts on me, she put her head down next to mine and in a breathy voice whispered something into my ear I won't repeat. "Here we go again," I thought to myself. Other women had put me in similar situations in the past, so while I temporarily froze, I wasn't totally shocked. Keep in mind that I had never flirted with this woman or encouraged this in any way. I was actually trying to hook her up with a friend, but he thought she was too sexy and would not be interested in him. It had taken me by complete surprise. Under normal circumstances this would be a dream come true for any man. She was a tall blond with an extremely beautiful face, wonderful, bubbly personality, and a smoking hot body. Going into her 50s and already a grandmother, she kept herself so well that she looked like she was in her late 30s. Most men in that situation would've loved it, so she proceeded with the assumption that it was welcomed behavior. I'm sure she never experienced rejection in her life when putting a man in this situation. I regret to say that I did not immediately push her back, but froze in position out of fear and excitement. She kissed me and started rubbing me. "I really like this," she whispered. After reaching up to her chest with my right hand (my left arm frozen in place), I decided to stop the situation as politely as I could. I attempted to talk a little bit with her to salvage the exchange of money, but within a few minutes I knew this wasn't going to happen. I was disappointed by my reaction as well as the money that would be lost since I didn't finish the lesson. After some awkward moments, I decided to quickly excuse myself. I literally ran out of the apartment. I was tired of this scenario. My discomfort at that moment showed me that I wanted to "forsake all others." After a conversation with my massage therapist—a wonderful woman named Shelle who acted like a real friend to me—I decided there would never be a perfect time when the stars would align and I would be magically ready for matrimony. There would always be temptations, fears, and risks. All I knew was that I never wanted to hurt Rebecca and that I couldn't imagine my life without her. While I felt sure I could be with any woman out there (single or otherwise, unfortunately), I wanted to be linked with the girl that had brought me so much peace, friendship, love, and kindness. I proposed to Rebecca that same week. Making that decision brought a lot of clarity and peace to my heart. I am grateful all the things that could have ruined our relationship did not. Many months later, Candy texted me out of the blue with some pretty flirtatious texts. I texted her that it was great to hear from her, but I was married now and probably shouldn't spend time with her alone. She never sent me another text after that. I feel only respect and admiration for her. During that brief episode, she knew I wasn't married, so anything was fair game. I respect her for not attempting to communicate with me after she found out I had committed. The only real commitment is marriage. While she made her move while I was dating—and I can't fault her for that—she did the right thing and left me alone without any drama after I married my wife. That's the way it should be. Whoever she ended up with should consider himself a truly lucky man, as I am. Your affectionate uncle, Tio Edwin

*"Why is it," he said, one time, at the subway entrance, "I feel
I've known you so many years?" "Because I like you," she said,
"and I don't want anything from you." —Ray Bradbury,
Fahrenheit 451.*

*If the full moon loves you, why worry about the stars? —African
proverb*

Dear Nephew,

Things are completely different with a woman that
can love you because of who she is, not because you have
to constantly inspire her to treat you well. I had been
friends with my wife for several years before I expressed a
romantic interest in her. The first time I approached her
directly, she rejected me. She had truly been the highlight
of my days towards the end of my previous relationship,
but she did not want to spend time alone since we were
both seeing other people. After I broke up with the previous
girlfriend, I had made the decision to not keep serial dating,
and gave myself the permission to go out with whoever I
wanted. My doctoral degree was almost finished and I
wanted to stop making the same mistakes over and over. A
few weeks after my break up, Rebecca and I discovered
that we had both broken up with our previous partners and
began seeing each other more regularly. I will never forget
the moment I knew my relationship with Rebecca was
headed towards marriage. It was towards the beginning of
our relationship. There was nothing complicated about it,
but I realized this woman was going to respect and love me

because that's who she intrinsically is. She told me how she felt about me seeing other girls by introducing me to the concept of boundaries, which was new to me at the time. This concept of boundaries was a clear way of articulating what had been slowly dawning on me in my dating relationships: clarity and honesty are the antidote to emotional heartbreak. This was the only discussion we ever had that could remotely be considered a fight, although she didn't raise her voice or put me down; she just described her feelings and told me how she wanted to feel. She looked at me with compassion and spoke calmly. She didn't understand my need to surround myself with so many women and knew that she couldn't do the same. She also knew that she enjoyed spending time with me and didn't want to stop. While she was concerned for my emotional well-being, she knew I had always been honest with her about seeing other people and saw I had been so hurt I didn't have much to give. Towards the end of our discussion, she said, "You give me what you can give me, and I will give you what I can give you. If the time comes when I can't give you any more, then I won't." I will never forget that moment. "You give me what you can give me, and I will give you what I can give you." Here finally was a woman owning her feelings, willing to keep me company even when I was unable to bend over backwards for her happiness. She was still living her life–getting ready to move out of the city, in fact–but was willing to continue spending time together. I had tried to accommodate the needs of so many girlfriends in the past that I was unwilling to constantly compromise my desires anymore. I didn't care what different social circles thought of my dating practices, especially after being treated so horribly when I broke up with the girlfriend before Rebecca. Those circles acted culturally and religiously superior, yet as soon as I did not meet their impossible expectations, they treated me like dirt and tried to hurt me, painting me as a predator. I couldn't care less what the "proper" way of dating or having a relationship was at this point. I had tried the proper way for well over a decade and it led to heartache and years wasted. My decision to follow my own desires in dating is one of the best decisions I ever made. I would pay attention to myself and follow my wants instead of pretending I was married. This wasn't me lying or cheating on women. Anyone who wanted to go out with me was not going to be exclusive, that was all. While this caused friction with some girls and indifference from others, Rebecca carried her own emotional weight. From the moment I met her, she focused on respecting me in a feminine manner. For example, our first get together (while we were still dating other people) she served me some rice she cooked herself, we briefly chatted, and then I excused myself. It was lovely how she treated others, even if she wasn't dating or interested in them. She did this not because I had earned it and jumped through hoops she created in her mind, but because that's who she is. Some phrases you'll hear from American girls are "You have to earn my respect" and "This relationship needs to be 50/50." The first time you hear something like that, run from that person and don't look back. The way you earn respect is by giving it, and it applies to both men and women. That means a good relationship is not 50/50, it's 100/100; both people treat the other with utmost respect and care because that's who they naturally are, not because the other person inspires them to act that way. At the end of that conversation, she asked me not to tell her which other women I was going out with; she didn't care to know. She was going to continue planning her life and career, but as long as we were in the same city, we would continue seeing each other as every time we would leave the encounter happier. She would enjoy the moment with me and, if we ended up not committing to each other long-term, she was at peace with that. To say she brought me peace would be a massive understatement. I'm constantly impressed by my wife's inner strength and kindness. She was kind when I couldn't make her feel like a princess. She focused on what she could give, what she could control, and her own behavior. I had spent hundreds of thousands of dollars and years trying to make past girlfriends feel special while disregarding my own desires. As soon as I decided to make myself a priority in life, this woman appeared who was kind, considerate, and strong. I learned a lot about myself during that brief period where I stopped going into pretend marriages. Most importantly, even after giving myself the permission to see other people, I found that I did not wish to part with her. Ever. I hope you will learn to focus, listen to, and understand your own feelings. As men we can be so focused on making women comfortable that we neglect our own desires, forgetting our feelings are equally as important as theirs. Especially while you are only dating, focus on what you want. Just like with those airplane instructions, before you can help someone else you have to be able to focus on helping yourself. In dating, I'm convinced, this means following your own desires and not those of the women around you. How can you know if you want to commit to someone if you have been neglecting your own feelings, fears, red flags, and desires the entire way? Focusing on what you want is the way that you can discover who you want to be with. Eventually you'll be able to focus on her like a laser, but at first you don't really know if you want her. Before that time, don't pretend to be married when you're not. With warm regards from your affectionate uncle, Tio Edwin.

All happy families are alike; each unhappy family is unhappy in its own way. —Leo Tolstoy, *Anna Karenina*

The most dangerous ideas in a society are not the ones being argued, but the ones that are assumed. —C.S. Lewis

Dear nephew,

While there is a lot to keep in mind when trying to find the woman you'll marry, I want to give you some general advice to conclude my letters to you on the subject. Filtering systems are a good way to keep the wrong people from entering your life. Politicians, celebrities, and upper management have filtering systems in order to keep people from bothering them and taking up their time. Why shouldn't we do the same? The best filtering systems are the people who love you. If your parents are willing to do it, I would start there. I am certainly going to do this for my children. When you meet a girl and have gone out with her a few times, before you ask her to be exclusive, ask your parents to meet her and her family a few times to see what they think. Ask them to be brutally honest. The goal is to cut people out of your life before there are problems. It's better to do this early rather than three years into an exclusive relationship that will leave you heartbroken. Your parents and family are the people who have known you the longest and love you most in this world. It would be wise to take their opinion into consideration. Another filtering system can be set up by small little rules you can have for yourself. We've already considered the idea of never seeing a woman twice before seeing another woman in order to keep the relationship intentionally non-exclusive. A fun idea to expand on this is that, upon meeting someone you're interested in or who might be interested in you, if you're in similar social circles, you could make a rule to never take her cell phone number or give yours out to someone you haven't spent significant time with. If done correctly, this would be a fun way to see if you guys actually want to spend time together. Rather than casually texting each other and randomly meeting up, both of you would have to find ways to see what events are happening that you could both attend, who is going, and make it work by planning ahead and having to talk in person. This forces the relationship to be intentional from the beginning, rather than falling into texting someone because you're bored and can't find someone else to hang with. I cringe at how many text conversations between young people of the opposite sex start with "Sup?" When you do end up going on a date with someone, if they are willing to go on a second date with you, always go out with them even if you don't like them. First impressions are not very reliable and it's always good to treat others how you would like to be treated. If after a few dates you know you will never have romantic feelings for a woman, rejecting a lady is never easy, but you must do it tactfully, respectfully, and decisively. Being truthful is always better. The clarity and simplicity that you will foster in your life by simply telling the truth will be priceless. Sometimes it's hard to know what you feel or think about something. The best way I've found to clarify my own thoughts is to write things down. Even if you don't keep a regular journal you will find that, when faced with any decision, writing down your thoughts will help immensely in clarifying how you feel about things. Even though I don't keep a journal, I do have daily planners that I write important events in. All I do is write a few words about the event in order to remember it later. When needing more space to write, I either go to a word document on a computer or a notebook. Even if it's just a few sentences, write it down and leave your thoughts there on the page. Coming back to it the next day will bring a lot more clarity to the situation. Something else that will help bring about clarity in your life is having an accountability partner. While this veers into the category of a spiritual practice, it is also a practical way to make sure that you have someone regularly to speak to about your activities with the opposite sex. Ideally this should be an older man who you admire and want to imitate. It's hard to find someone to hold you accountable given that it's such a time commitment, but one good place to start would be an older man from church who you admire. If you are close with your father, even better. Ask him. If you live far away, someone who is near you might be the best way to go. My father has held me accountable in the past and those were invaluable times where he helped me grow as a man. I've also had a few accountability partners when I lived in different states who were crucial in my personal growth. Going up to a pastor, bible study leader, or any other older man you admire is not as hard as it might seem. Avoid having people your same age or younger as accountability partners. While it would be more comfortable, your talks can easily devolve into gossip or just having fun rather than being a space to be challenged and grow. I hope I've given you plenty to work on in these letters about women and dating. As I mentioned before, between girlfriends and other romantic relationships, I had more than 40 love interests before meeting my wife. I've shared some of the stories from my life here because I would love for you to avoid my mistakes and build on my successes. This is one of the most important aspects of your life, and in spite of how movies and the rest of the culture treat the topic, I'm glad you're taking women and dating seriously. You won't regret it. Your affectionate uncle, Tio Edwin.

Thank you for reading *Dear Nephew... by Tio Edwin.*

For coaching, speaking engagements, or special appearance inquiries, please email us at TioEdwinCoaching@gmail.com.